Hellenistic Religions

HELLENISTIC RELIGIONS

An Introduction

Luther H. Martin

New York   Oxford
OXFORD UNIVERSITY PRESS
1987

Oxford University Press

Oxford   New York   Toronto
Delhi   Bombay   Calcutta   Madras   Karachi
Petaling Jaya   Singapore   Hong Kong   Tokyo
Nairobi   Dar es Salaam   Cape Town
Melbourne   Auckland

and associated companies in
Beirut   Berlin   Ibadan   Nicosia

Library of Congress Cataloging-in-Publication Data
Martin, Luther H., 1937–
Hellenistic religions.
Bibliography: p.
Includes index.
1. Religion—History.   2. Hellenism.   I. Title.
BL722.M33   1987   291'.0938   86-31281
ISBN 0-19-504390-1
ISBN 0-19-504391-X (pbk.)

1 3 5 7 9 8 6 4 2

Printed in the United States of America
on acid-free paper

To my Mother and Father

Preface

When one pursues an education in an area of inquiry, which for one reason or another has caught his fancy, he is presented with an astonishing array of information, along with some irksome problems of understanding, many of which linger long into his career of teaching and scholarship. One longs for some sort of synthetic overview and for modest attempts to answer perennial questions. This book is an attempt to understand as a coherent system of thought the profusion of data usually collated under the rubric "Hellenistic Religion." Its synthetic and systemic treatment of the material, rather than being exhaustive or specialized, will I hope prove useful as an introduction as well as a framework for further study.

This book evolved during a generation of teaching undergraduates at The University of Vermont, and I am indebted to my students for their reactions, suggestions, and insights concerning much of the material that follows. Because of its genesis in an undergraduate context and its intended nonspecialist readership, the selected bibliographies at the ends of the chapters are limited primarily to available English language works, with apologies to my European colleagues. Their important contributions to the study of Hellenistic religions are documented in such comprehensive bibliographies as those of Bruce Metzger on "Greco-Roman Mystery Religions" in *Aufstieg und Niedergang der Römischen Welt* (II, 17. 3, Berlin and New York: Walter de Gruyter, 1984), as well as in the continuing specialized contributions to this series, and of David Scholar on "Nag Hammadi" (Leiden: E. J. Brill, 1971 and updated annually in *Novum Testamentum*), the gnostic manuscript discovery which has produced a wealth of scholarship.

Citations of classical sources are from the translations of the Loeb Classical Library (Harvard University Press) when available; biblical passages are from the Revised Standard Version unless otherwise noted; and the Nag Hammadi gnostic texts are from the translations edited by James M. Robinson (*The Nag Hammadi Library,* San Francisco: Harper, 1977).

Some of the material used in this book was previously published and is used here by permission:

"Josephus' Use of *Heimarmene* in the *Jewish Antiquities* XIII, 171–73." *Numen* XXVII, 2 (1981).

"Why Cecropian Minerva? Hellenistic Religious Syncretism as System." *Numen* XXX, 2 (1983).

"Those Elusive Eleusinian Mystery Shows." *Helios,* Spring (1986).

"Identity and Self-Knowledge in the Syrian Thomas Tradition." *Identity Issues and World Religions: Selected Proceedings of the Fifteenth Congress of the International Association for the History of Religion,* ed. Victor C. Hayes (Bedford Park, South Australia: Australian Association for the Study of Religion, 1986), pp. 34–41.

"Divination, Interpretation and Dreams." *The Second Century,* forthcoming.

I am indebted also to numerous colleagues who have read this manuscript, in whole or in part, at various stages of its writing. In particular, I would like to thank Wayne Rollins for the encouragement he gave me to begin the project, and James Goss, Mary Hall, and William Paden for their encouragement in continuing the project.

Especially, I would like to thank my wife, Rux, for the extraordinary patience and care she brought to the reading of numerous drafts of this work—her keen editorial eye has saved it from many infelicities of expression.

Underhill Center, Vermont   L. H. M.
May 1987

Contents

Abbreviations of Classical Sources Cited

Apuleius (c. 123–after 161 c.e.)
Apol.: Apologia
Met.: Metamorphoses (The Golden Ass)

Aristotle (384–322 b.c.e.)
Metaph.: Metaphysica

Cicero (106–43 b.c.e.)
Div.: De Divinatione

Cleanthes (331–232 b.c.e.)
Hymn to Zeus: From Stobaeus *Eclogae* I, 1. 12

Clement of Alexandria (c. 150–between 211–216 c.e.)
Exc. Thdt.: Excerpta Theodoti
Protr.: Protrepticus

CH: Corpus Hermeticum

CMC: Cologne Mani Codex

Diod. Sic.: Diodorus Siculus (first century b.c.e.)

Diog. Laert.: Diogenes Laertius (first half of the third century c.e.)

Epictetus (c. 55–c. 185 c.e.)
Ench.: Enchiridion (Manual)

EPICURUS (341–270 B.C.E.)
Ep. Men.: Letter to Menoeceus from *Diog. Laert.*, Bk. 10

EURIPIDES (C. 485–C. 406 B.C.E.)
Bacch.: The Bacchae

Hdt.: Herodotus (fifth century B.C.E.)

HIPPOLYTUS (C. 170–C. 236 C.E.)
Haer.: Refutatio Omnium Haeresium

HOMER
Il.: Illiad
Od.: Odyssey

Hymn Hom.: Homeric Hymn to
Cer.: Cererem (Demeter)
Herm.: Hermes
Bacch.: Bacchum (Dionysus)

IG: Inscriptiones Graecae

IRENAEUS (C. 130–C. 200 C.E.)
Haer.: Adversus Haereses

JEROME (C. 342–420 C.E.)
Ep.: Epistulae

JOSEPHUS (37/38–C. 100 C.E.)
AJ: Antiquitates Judaicae

LUCIAN (C. 120–AFTER 180 C.E.)
Alex.: Alexander
Salt.: De Saltatione
Syr. D.: De Syria Dea

NHC: Nag Hammadi Codices

ORIGEN (185/186–254/255 C.E.)
C. Cel.: Contra Celsum

OVID (43 B.C.E.–17 C.E.)
Ars Am.: Ars Amatoria (The Lover's Handbook)

Paus.: Pausanias (mid-second century C.E.)

PGM: Papryi Graecae Magicae

PINDAR (518–438 B.C.E.)
Nem.: Nemean Odes
Ol.: Olympian Odes

PLATO (C. 429–347 B.C.E.)
Resp.: Respublica

PLINY (THE ELDER) (23/24–79 C.E.)
HN: Naturalis Historia

PLINY (THE YOUNGER) (C. 61–C. 112 C.E.)
Tra.: Epistulae ad Traianum

PHILO (C. 20 B.C.E.–C. 50 C.E.)
Cher: De Cherubim (On the Cherubim)
Cont.: De Vita Contemplativa (On the Contemplative Life)
Fug.: De Fuga et Inventione (On Flight and Finding)
Her.: Quis Rerum Divinarum Heres (Who Is the Heir)
Mig.: De Migratione Abrahami (On the Migration of Abraham)

PLOTINUS (205–269/90 C.E.)
Enn.: Enneades

PLUTARCH (BEFORE 50–AFTER 120 C.E.)
Cons. ad Uxor.: Consolatio ad Uxorem
De Alex. Fort.: De Fortuna Alexandri (On Alexander's Fortune)
De Frat. Amor.: De Fraterno Amore (On Brotherly Love)
De Is. et Os.: De Iside et Osiride
Vit. Alc.: Vitae Parallelae Alcibiades (Life of Alcibiades)
Vit. Pomp.: Vitae Parallelae Pompeius (Life of Pompey)
Vit. Sol.: Vitae Parallelae Solon (Life of Solon)

PORPHYRY (232/233–C. 305 C.E.)
De Antr. Nymph.: De Antro Nympharum (The Cave of the Nymphs)

PTOLEMY (MID-SECOND CENTURY C.E.)
Tet.: Tetrabiblos

SENECA (THE YOUNGER) (4 B.C.E.–65 C.E.)
Ep.: Epistulae

SUETONIUS (C. 69–AFTER 122 C.E.)
Ner.: Nero

TACITUS (C. 56–AFTER 115 C.E.)
Ann.: Annales

TERTULLIAN (C. 160–C. 220 C.E.)
Adv. Valent.: Adversus Valentinianos

Thuc.: Thucydides (c. 460–c. 400 B.C.E.)

Hellenistic Religions

Introduction

"I seek God!" cried the wandering madman of Nietzsche's famous parable. But in response to his own rhetorical question, he proclaimed throughout the marketplace that the creator of world order in the Christian West was dead.[1] At the very least, in the view of Martin Heidegger, one of Nietzsche's greatest commentators, God is silent, withdrawn, and no longer responsive to the human condition.[2]

It is no longer novel to see the modern condition as parallel to that of the Hellenistic age.[3] Both are shaped in periods of transformation characterized by explosions in knowledge of the physical world signaled by cosomological revolution, by altered sociopolitical systems, by dramatic encounters with cultures once located beyond the boundaries of civilization, by religious reformations and the influx of strange new gods from the East. For both, the traditional gods might well be termed dead.

Modern assumptions regarding human existence were shaped by the Renaissance rediscovery of ancient culture.[4] This revival in learning was mediated by the Hellenistic attempt to comprehend the realities of human nature and the world, itself based upon the traditions of Moses and Homer. The Hellenistic world therefore not only provides a historical paradigm for understanding the modern order of things, but is also a medium—the soil, as it were, in which the formative roots of Western culture, both Hebraic and Hellenic, were preserved and cultivated from antiquity to the Renaissance.

The Hellenistic Age

A Hellenistic period was first defined in the mid-nineteenth century, in terms of the "great man" view of history,[5] as the age extending from the conquests of Alexander the Great in the early fourth century B.C.E. to the annexation of Egypt into the Roman Empire by Augustus in 30 B.C.E.[6] In 336, Alexander (356–323 B.C.E.) succeeded his father to the Macedonian throne when he was only twenty years old. By the time of his death thirteen years later, his passion to unite the Greek peoples against Persian power had resulted in an empire that extended from the Aegean eastward to the Indus River in India, and from the northern shores of the Black Sea and the banks of the Danube south to Nubia and the Sahara in northern Africa (see Figure 1). The goal of this young student of Aristotle was to transform the diverse local peoples in the eastern Mediterranean area and those of western Asia into a universal empire, unified by Greek language and culture. His empire irreversibly altered the sociopolitical world of the Greeks by replacing the local world of the polis, the Hellenic model of the independent, democratic city-state, with an internationalizing vision of the entire world as polis.

To a great extent, the realization of Alexander's cosmopolitan ideal depended not so much upon the advances of Greek civilization as upon the charismatic genius of the emperor himself, and with his death the nascent empire soon broke apart. At the Battle of Ipsus in 301 B.C.E., Antigonus of Phrygia, the last of Alexander's generals, died defending the imperial dream. With him fell any possibility of retaining the political unity of the empire. As one scholar summarizes the complex events that followed:

> That world presently returned very much to the political shape it had before Alexander, though under different rulers and a different civilization. By 275 three dynasties, descended from three of his [Alexander's] generals, were well established; the Seleucids ruled much of what had been the Persian empire in Asia, the Ptolemies ruled Egypt, and the Antigonids Macedonia. A fourth European dynasty, not connected with Alexander, the Attalids of Pergamum, subsequently grew up in Asia Minor at Seleucid expense, and became great by favour of Rome. In 212 Rome began to take part, at first tentatively, in Hellenistic affairs, and ultimately absorbed the whole Mediterranean world, the last independent state, Egypt, coming to an end in 30 B.C.[7]

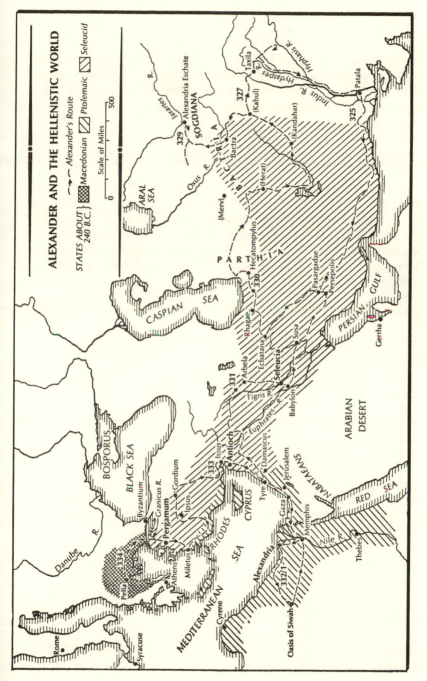

ALEXANDER AND THE HELLENISTIC WORLD

STATES ABOUT 240 B.C.

Alexander's Route

Macedonian

Ptolemaic

Seleucid

Scale of Miles

0   500

Rome

Syracuse

Pella

Byzantium

BOSPORUS

BLACK SEA

Danube R.

Athens

Granicus R.

Gordium

Miletus

Ipsus

Pergamum

RHODES

CYPRUS

MEDITERRANEAN SEA

Cyrene

Alexandria

Oasis of Siwah

Memphis

Thebes

Nile R.

RED SEA

NABATAEANS

Gaza

Jerusalem

Tyre

Damascus

Antioch

Issus

Euphrates R.

Tigris R.

Babylon

Seleucia

Arbela

Ecbatana

Susa

Rhagae

ARABIAN DESERT

Gerrha

PERSIAN GULF

Pasargadae

Persepolis

PARTHIA

Hecatompylus

CASPIAN SEA

ARAL SEA

Oxus R.

Jaxartes R.

(Merv)

(Herat)

BACTRIA

Bactra

SOGDIANA

Alexandria Eschate

(Kabul)

(Kandahar)

Taxila

Indus R.

Hydaspes R.

Hyphasis R.

Patala

334

333

332/1

331

330

329

327

325

Figure 1

The date 30 B.C.E. marks the final incorporation into the Roman empire of the lands once ruled by Alexander and is a convenient mark for the end of a Hellenistic and the beginning of a Roman period of political history; but a Hellenistic cultural history cannot be so sharply distinguished.[8] Although the influence of Hellenistic culture extended until the Renaissance, a study of Hellenistic religion must be concluded with the fourth century C.E., for this century witnessed both the conversion of the Roman Emperor Constantine to Christianity in 313, and the imperial decrees of Theodosius I in 380 founding the orthodox Christian state and in 391 finally prohibiting paganism and closing the temples.[9] This official acceptance and legitimization at the end of the fourth century of one religious possibility effectively signals the beginning of a new religious jurisdiction. The term "Hellenistic" will be used to designate the religious forms and practices of the many peoples who found themselves inhabitants of the expanded world inaugurated by Alexander's empire, up until the emergence of a Christian world.

The Hellenistic World

At the same time that a new internationalism was expanding political and cultural possibilities throughout the entire eastern Mediterranean area, a cosmological revolution was occurring.[10] The new cosmology that emerged was later named after Claudius Ptolemy (circa 100–178 C.E.), who gave it systematic formulation.

Western culture has occupied only three cosmic structures: the classical cosmos of the ancient Near Eastern and Greek civilizations with its threefold hierarchy of heaven, earth, and underworld; the greatly expanded and differentiated Ptolemaic cosmic image which replaced the classical one at the beginning of the Hellenistic period and endured until the Renaissance; and the modern Copernican cosmos.[11] The significance of the Ptolemaic revolution cannot be fully appreciated apart from a brief consideration of the classical cosmology that preceded it.

The classical cosmic image is sketched by the Greek dramatist Euripides (circa 485–406 B.C.E.):

> Heaven and Earth were once one form, and when they had been
> separated from one another, they gave birth and brought up into the

light all things: trees, birds, beasts, and spawn of the sea, and race
of mortals.   Frag. 484, *Melanippe*[12]

This cosmogonic image of primordial formlessness, of the separation
of a personified Father Heaven and a Mother Earth, and of the
subsequent sexual generation of all things pervaded the myths of the
early Mesopotamian and Egyptian river civilizations as well as the
writings of Homer and Hesiod. According to Aristotle (*Metaph.*
983b), Thales "declared that the earth rests on water."[13] The image
of the earth as a flat disk buoyed on the primordial formless water
from which it had emerged was common to the ancient Near Eastern
and Hellenic cultures. Under the surface of this disk was the underworld; over it arched the heaven.

Traditionally, an integrated view of the cosmos was maintained
by means of pious homage to the gods at the center of the world,
whether that center was marked cosmically by the sacred mountain,
home of the gods, or in cult by the *omphalos* or navel of the world, as
the Greeks termed it. This cosmic center designated the reference for
locating the four cardinal points of the compass. At the same time,
the center, as axis of the world, linked the zenith of the cosmic realm
with its nadir, thus bringing the total cosmos into geometric harmony.
To the extent that they existed in proximity to this center, humans
were at home with the gods within the protecting and nourishing
womb of a contained and containing cosmos, dwelling in "umbilical"
filiation with their world. As Homer wrote, "earth and high Olympus
remain yet common to us all" (*Il.* 15, 195).

This traditional cosmology was first challenged by the sixth-
century B.C.E. pre-Socratic philosophers, who replaced mythological
images with abstract Ionian physical ideas and Pythagorean mathematical forms. The philosopher and astronomer Anaximander (611–
547 B.C.E.), for example, suggested that the earth was an unsupported
cylinder suspended in the middle of the universe. The Pythagorean
vision of a planetary order provided the background for an image of
the earth surrounded by concentric planetary spheres, an image elaborated in the fourth century B.C.E. by Plato's student Eudoxus (circa
390–340 B.C.E.). Such Greek innovations, together with Babylonian
and Egyptian astronomy, contributed to the general acceptance of a
new "unified picture" of the cosmos at the dawn of the Hellenistic
period.[14]

Although Ptolemaic cosmology retained the geocentricity of the
traditional image, the celestial bounds of the classical image were

extended to a distant realm of fixed stars that embraced seven differentiated planetary spheres surrounding the earth. From a geocentric perspective, the moon was the closest of the planets to the earth, and Saturn was the most distant. Mercury, Venus, Sun, Mars, and Jupiter occupied positions two, three, four, five and six respectively (see Figure 2). The terrestrial, sublunar realm was sharply separated from the celestial, superlunar realm by an abyss of cosmic space populated by elemental and demonic powers. These powers controlled the terrestrial realm, even as they in turn were controlled by the celestial deities.[15] This new architecture of the cosmos, together with the new international political topography, defined the hierarchical and horizontal framework of a Hellenistic world system and structured the religious forms distinctive to it.[16]

Religion in the Hellenistic World

Homer's tales of a family of Olympian deities who are associated with the polis and its underlying familial values remain one of the formative elements not only of Greek but of all Western civilization. The transformation of the sociopolitical world after Alexander and of the traditional cosmic image was paralleled in Greece and elsewhere by a transformation of religious forms. Under the influence of Greek philosophical rationalism, the meaning of such tales as those of Homer began to be questioned. By the fifth century B.C.E., the Greek poet Pindar (518–438 B.C.E.) had distinguished between the historic tale (*logos*) and the poetic tale (*mythos*) (*Ol.* I, 28–29, and *Nem.* VII, 23). On the one hand, the Hellenistic Stoic philosophers understood the polytheistic *mythos* as an allegorical expression of a single, universal, and natural reality (*logos*) underlying the diversity of religious expression. On the other hand, the fourth-century mythographer Euhemerus suggested that the mythic tales of divine exploits preserved legends of ancient heroes, thus effectively subsuming *mythos* to the criterion of a historical *logos*.[17]

At the same time, an earlier chthonic (from the Greek *chthon,* meaning earth; of the underworld and its spirits) evocation of sacrality began to flourish in place of the relocated celestial sacrality. The ancient festival of Demeter, goddess of grain, celebrated at Eleusis, enjoyed renewed popularity in the Hellenistic world and survived well into the period of Roman decline; and the orgiastic frenzies of Dionysus, the very embodiment of chthonic spirit, swept the Hellenistic world.

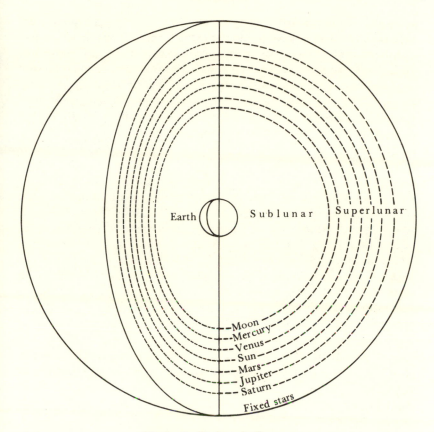

Figure 2. Ptolemaic Cosmos

Traditional Olympian religion, associated as it was with the polis, belonged to the established sociopolitical order. One was born in a particular locale and into its particular religion. As a citizen of Athens, for example, one was devoted to the goddess Athena. Chthonic religion, however, was a response to the spontaneity of the sacred, a voluntary association of individuals that embodied an implicit challenge to the official sociopolitical order. Whereas the fundamental characteristic of the Olympians was their transcendence, that is, their superiority to and control over human affairs, a more direct relationship was possible between the chthonic deities and their human suppliants. Humans still inhabited the center of the cosmic womb, but the classical image of heroic quest through a world directly ruled by the gods was replaced by the Hellenistic image of fortuitous wandering through a labyrinthian terrestrial realm from which the gods were absent. The chthonic deities had departed from the terrestrial realm—characterized by Ptolemy as chaotic, subject to constant and unpredictable change (*Tet.* I, 1)—and had gone to their now distant celestial thrones; they were separated from humans by the chasm of sublunar space. More than the waning Olympian mode, this universalized chthonic expression of sacrality carried Greek influence into the uncharted transformations of the Hellenistic world.

Syncretism or System

With the advent of Hellenistic internationalism, Eastern deities, such as the Egyptian Isis and the Syrian Atargatis, found themselves welcomed as cultural citizens of Hellenistic society and worshipped alongside traditional Greek deities by a newly constituted cosmopolitan following. As these once localized deities, Greek and non-Greek, met in the international arena, an inevitable process of interaction took place that necessitated a transformation of their role and a resituation of their place in the cosmos. As these deities gradually became participants in the Hellenistic world, they were simultaneously severed from their original roles and meanings. Increasingly, the different deities became understood as aspects of a common Hellenistic religious system rather than expressions of historically discrete traditions.[18]

This cultural interaction is usually termed "syncretism" and has become accepted as "the main characteristic feature of Hellenistic religion."[19] Based upon an oft-cited but incorrect etymology (from the Greek *synkerannumi,* meaning to mix or join together), the notion of syncretism is derived from the political model of Hellenistic culture as the mixture of peoples resulting from Alexander's conquests.[20] As such, it defines Hellenistic religion as a response to the new political internationalism, a response that preserved the richness and particularity of tradition so vital to religious understanding.

The political understanding of syncretism neglects, however, the systemic dimension of Hellenistic religions suggested by the common architecture of their cosmic arena. Interpreting Hellenistic religions as responses of traditional religions to the cultural situation created by Alexander's empire is much too simplistic for so rich and complex a subject. It is not useful to understand any coherently identifiable cultural form as grounded in superficial borrowings occasioned by circumstantial contact. Syncretism, so conceived, describes the problem of understanding Hellenistic religions rather than explaining the common structures of thought that allowed the various religious expressions of the Hellenistic world.

In the ancient world, however, syncretism is the term used by Plutarch to describe the reconciliation of the normally factious Cretans in the face of attack by a foreign foe,

> who, though they often quarrelled with and warred against each other, made up their differences and united when outside enemies attacked; and this it was which they called "syncretism."
>
> *De Frat. Amor.* 19

Plutarch thus employed the term to signify a system of relationships defined by resemblances and organized by the play of sympathy and antipathy.

Like the shared architecture of Hellenistic cosmology, syncretism in the Plutarchian sense suggests the possibility of understanding religion in the Hellenistic age as a coherent system rather than as the fortuitous byproduct of political internationalism. Hellenistic religious syncretism may best point to coherent patterns of relationships that must be described in their systemic particulars, rather than a cultural mixture born of historical happenstance.

Piety, Mystery, Gnosis

The Hellenistic world distinguished among three types of discourse and practice that are usually grouped under the singular category of "religious": piety, mystery, and gnosis. These three types assumed an essentially identical order of things but evaluated this order differently; consequently, they represent three different strategies of existence.

Piety (in Greek, *eusebeia*; in Latin, *pietas*) signifies reverence, honor, or esteem, especially in social and legal relationships, such as proper behavior between a man and his wife, a slave and his master, or legions and their commander. It also signifies right relations between mortals and the immortals. Piety, then, designates the traditional system of conventional practices concerning the home and family and, by extension, those practices which surround and are part of being at home in one's world under the rule of a family of gods. Although similar practices of piety are recognizable in many different cultures and in various historical periods, they are always articulated in terms of a particular locale or place and are transmitted through local tradition. They represent the expression by a particular people of their local order of things. The practice of piety assumes that knowledge of this order of things is self-evident and available to the populace apart from divine intervention or institutional mediation, although the assistance of a "specialist" may be helpful. This assumption of an order of things manifest in everyday life is more than anything else characteristic of piety. Representing a locally situated strategy of existence, the techniques and practices of piety precede or underlie historically founded or transplanted religious traditions.

Like the practices of piety, the Hellenistic Mysteries also assumed a systemic order of things. However, they did not assume that this order was readily accessible and sought to remedy for their initiates this deficiency in the received order. By the Hellenistic period, the term "mystery" designated not only certain classical Greek cults but increasingly Eastern cults that spread west under the favorable conditions of empire. Silence surrounded all the "Mysteries," a word that derives from the Greek verb *myō,* meaning "to shut the eyes" or "to keep one's mouth shut," especially "in fear of danger" or, by extension, "in the face of awe."

Gnosis designates any teaching in which salvation depends upon knowledge (in Greek, *gnōsis*) rather than upon ritual practices. It is a revealed, self-realized spiritual knowledge held to be deeper and more profound than that available to the intellectual or philosophical inquiry (in Greek, *epistēmē*) which had been developing in Greece since the sixth century B.C.E. As such, it characterizes such disparate traditions as that of the Upanishads (the knowledge *tat tvam asi*) and *jnana* yoga (the yoga of knowledge) in India, knowledge of the Buddha nature or of the Tao in the Far East, and the initiatory knowledge of the Mysteries, as well as the radical strategies of individual existence known as Gnosticism that swept the late Hellenistic world.

The following survey will examine Hellenistic religions in terms of these three strategies of existence, inquiring into their characteristic forms and expressions, their differences and relationships, and their place in a Hellenistic system of religious thought.

Notes

1. Walter Kaufmann (trans.), *The Gay Science,* in *The Portable Nietzsche* (New York: Viking, 1954), pp. 95–96; see also *The Gay Science: Book V,* addition to the 2nd ed. (1887), pp. 447–450.

2. Douglas Scott (trans.), "Remembrance of the Poet," in *Existence and Being* (Chicago: Henry Regnery, 1949), pp. 243–269.

3. See, for example, the philosopher Hans Jonas, "Epilogue," in *The Gnostic Religion,* 2nd ed. (Boston: Beacon Press, 1963), pp. 320–340; the psychologist Rollo May in an interview in the *New York Times,* November 25, 1968; and the historian of religion Robert S. Ellwood, Jr., *Religious and Spiritual Groups in Modern America* (Englewood Cliffs, N.J.: Prentice-Hall, 1973), pp. 43–54.

4. See, for example, Jean Seznec, *The Survival of the Pagan Gods: The Mythological Tradition and Its Place in Renaissance Humanism and Art,* trans. Barbara F. Sessions (New York: Harper & Row, 1961); Frances Yates, *Giordano Bruno and the Hermetic Tradition* (New York: Random House, 1969); and Edgar Wind, *Pagan Mysteries in the Renaissance,* rev. ed. (New York: Norton, 1968).

5. Robert Stover, "Great Man Theory of History," in Paul Edwards (ed.), *The Encyclopedia of Philosophy,* vol. 3 (New York: Macmillan, 1972), pp. 378–382.

6. J. G. Droysen, *Geschichte des Hellenismus,* 3 vols. (1836–43, 2nd ed. 1877); rev. ed. by E. Bayer (Munich: Deutscher Taschenbuch, 1952–1953; reprinted 1980).

7. W. W. Tarn and G. T. Griffith, *Hellenistic Civilization,* 3rd ed. (New York: New American Library, 1961), p. 6.

8. See, for example, the rather laborious discussion by F. C. Grant, *Hellenistic Religions: The Age of Syncretism,* in The Library of Liberal Arts (Indianapolis, Ind.: Bobbs-Merrill, 1953), pp. xi–xiii.

9. Jonathan Z. Smith, "Hellenistic Religions," in *The Encyclopedia Brittanica,* 15th ed. (Chicago: University of Chicago Press, 1985), "Macropaedia," vol. 18, pp. 925–927.

10. "Cosmology" is used not in the modern philosophical sense to designate a branch of metaphysics but is used in a descriptive sense to designate a model or physical image of the universe.

11. Milton K. Munitz (ed.), *Theories of the Universe from Babylonian Myth to Modern Science* (New York: Free Press, 1957), provides a useful anthology of Western cosmological theory.

12. Augustus Nauch (ed., with supplement ed. Bruno Snell), *Tragicorum Graecorum Fragmenta* (Hildesheim, Germany: Georg Olms, 1964), p. 511.

13. G. E. R. Lloyd, *Polarity and Analogy: Two Types of Argumentation in Early Greek Thought* (Cambridge: Cambridge University Press, 1966), p. 306.

14. Samuel Sambursky, *The Physical World of Late Antiquity* (New York: Basic Books, 1962), p. 133.

15. Franz Cumont, *Astrology and Religion Among the Greeks and Romans,* trans. J. B. Baker (New York: Dover, 1960), p. 68.

16. The importance of Ptolemaic cosmology for understanding Hellenistic religion in the face of its complexity and seeming contradictions is emphasized by Martin P. Nilsson, *Geschichte der Griechischen Religion,* vol. II, 2nd ed. (Munchen: C. H. Beck, 1961–1967), pp. 702–711. See also E. R. Dodds, *Pagan and Christian in an Age of Anxiety* (New York: Norton, 1970), chap. 1.

17. Jean Seznec, pp. 11–12.

18. Jonathan Z. Smith, "Native Cults in the Hellenistic Period," *History of Religions* XI (1971), pp. 236–249.

19. F. C. Grant, p. xiii.

20. Used in this sense, the characterization of Hellenistic religion as "syncretistic" goes back to the work of Droysen. For an account of religious opposition to Hellenism, see Samuel K. Eddy, *The King is Dead: Studies in the Near Eastern Resistance to Hellenism 334–31 B.C.* (Lincoln, Neb.: University of Nebraska Press, 1961).

Selected Bibliography

Alexander

N. G. L. Hammond, *Alexander the Great: King, Commander and Statesman* (Park Ridge, N.J.: Noyes Press, 1980).

W. W. Tarn, *Alexander the Great,* 2 vols. (Chicago: Ares, 1981), is the classic study in English.

C. Bradford Welles, *Alexander and the Hellenistic World* (Toronto: A. M. Hakkert, 1970).

Hellenistic History and Culture

Erich S. Gruen, *The Hellenistic World and the Coming of Rome,* 2 vols. (Berkeley, Calif.: University of California Press, 1984).

Moses Hadas, *Hellenistic Culture: Fusion and Diffusion* (New York: Norton, 1972).

F. E. Peters, *The Harvest of Hellenism: A History of the Near East from Alexander the Great to the Triumph of Christianity* (New York: Simon and Schuster, 1970), has a good working bibliography.

W. W. Tarn and G. T. Griffith, *Hellenistic Civilization,* 3rd ed. (New York: New American Library, 1961).

F. W. Walbank, *The Hellenistic World* (Cambridge, Mass.: Harvard University Press, 1982).

Polis

Gustave Glotz, *The Greek City and Its Institutions* (New York: Knopf, 1951) is the classic study of the Greek polis.

A. H. M. Jones, *The Greek City: From Alexander to Justinian* (Oxford: Clarendon Press, 1940).

Hellenistic Religions

H. Idris Bell, *Cults and Creeds in Graeco-Roman Egypt* (Chicago: Ares, 1975).

E. R. Dodds, *Pagan and Christian in an Age of Anxiety* (New York: Norton, 1970).

John Ferguson, *The Religions of the Roman Empire* (Ithaca, N.Y.: Cornell University Press, 1970).

F. C. Grant, *Hellenistic Religions: The Age of Syncretism,* in The Library of Liberal Arts (Indianapolis, Ind.: Bobbs-Merrill, 1953), is a collection of texts for the study of religion in this period.

Martin P. Nilsson, *Geschichte der Griechischen Religion* (vol. I, 3rd ed.; vol. II, 2nd ed.) (Munich: C. H. Beck, 1961–1967), is the most comprehensive account of Hellenistic religion; vol. II is devoted to the religions of the Hellenistic and Roman period.

A. D. Nock, *Conversion: The Old and the New in Religion from Alexander the Great to Augustine of Hippo* (London: Oxford University Press, 1961), offers a perceptive overview of Hellenistic religion in terms of this one theme.

Cultural Influence of Hellenistic Religions

Jean Seznec, *The Survival of the Pagan Gods: The Mythological Tradition and Its Place in Renaissance Humanism and Art,* trans. Barbara F. Sessions (New York: Harper & Row, 1961).

Edgar Wind, *Pagan Mysteries in the Renaissance,* rev. ed. (New York: Norton, 1968).

Frances Yates, *Giordano Bruno and the Hermetic Tradition* (New York: Random House, 1969).

1

The Golden Ass in a Labyrinthian World

Any attempt to understand religion in the Hellenistic world does well to begin with the *Metamorphoses,* that great erotic novel of the mid-second century C.E. by the philosopher and rhetorician Lucius Apuleius (circa 123–after 161).[1] *The Golden Ass,* as it is better known, is a morality tale that juxtaposes hedonistic existence in the Hellenistic world with the peace, joy, and blessedness of the religious life. As a piece of religious propaganda, it "sums up its epoch."[2] Its vivid descriptions of the world and intertwined mythic themes must have had to ring true if its alternative of salvation were to appeal.[3] Perhaps more than any other single text, this fantastic and lusty story surveys the conditions of everyday life in the Hellenistic world.

The novel opens with Lucius, a sort of Hellenistic Everyman, journeying on business to Hypata in Thessaly, a region in eastern Greece renowned as a center of magic and as the home of witches (*Met.* II, 1). While in Hypata, Lucius is the guest of Milo, a friend of a friend. When he discovers that his host's wife, Pamphile, is a sorceress, and that her servant girl, Fotis, welcomes his amorous advances, Lucius indulges his curiosity about both women and magic, despite warnings to the contrary. Having seduced Fotis, and with her assistance, he secretly observes Pamphile transform herself into an owl and fly off to an erotic rendezvous. When Lucius insists on trying the

magic ointment himself, Fotis in her haste selects the wrong ointment, and Lucius is transformed into an ass.

As the consequence of his meddling with women and magic,
Lucius must undertake a deceptively simple quest for the transformative antidote, the common rose. His asinine wanderings, however,
lead him through a cross section of the Hellenistic world, a labyrinth
of lawlessness and danger, magic and divination, strange festivals and
bizarre rituals, degrading servitude and pornographic exploitation,
until he is delivered from his fate by divine intervention. Apuleius's
description of the appearance of the goddess Isis to Lucius in a
dream, of his final transformation back into a human by eating the
garland of roses carried by a priest of Isis in a cultic procession, and of
his subsequent initiation into the Mysteries of the goddess is a major
source of knowledge about Hellenistic religion.[4]

The Fictive World of Apuleius

Just as Alexander's political ideal of empire defined the parameters
of Hellenistic civilization and the Ptolemaic image of planetary
spheres circumscribed a cosmic order, so Apuleius's novel constitutes
a narrative field of inclusion. It contains a series of framed tales
within framed tales, each mirroring the others, and its conclusion
turns back on the opening to transform the meaning of the entire
book. The episodes in the novel are thus parts of an interconnected
whole. By the conclusion, the reader is no longer confused by the
seemingly arbitrary structure of the novel, even as Lucius is no longer
confined to a life of fortuitous wandering.

Although the magical means and hedonistic ends of Pamphile,
Fotis, and Lucius at first seem to contrast moralistically with the
spiritual existence of Isis and her initiates, they are finally revealed to
be the necessary motivation for the novel's soteriological drama and
part of the providential plan of the deity. Indeed, the meaning of
Apuleius's novel comes fully to life only in the context of its concluding account of divine epiphany. In retrospect, the strange and charming tales overheard by the eavesdropping ass during his wanderings
reveal an interrelated structure to the "eavesdropping" reader.

The well-known tale of Psyche and Eros, which lies at the very
center of the novel, provides an example of this "revealed" meaning.
The ass, Lucius, overhears an old woman telling this tale to cheer up
a young bride who, like the ass, has been abducted by a band of

robbers. In the tale Psyche, the youngest daughter of the king and queen, is considered so beautiful that she is often compared with Venus. Fearing that she might become vain, the king consults the oracle of Apollo, which pronounces that Psyche must leap from a craggy height into a "marriage of death" with Eros. Carried by the winds into the valley below, Psyche enters the marvelous house of the god where her every desire is magically provided. But only by night does the invisible god arrive to consummate the marriage, warning her that she must never see him. Overcome by curiosity, however, Psyche lights a lamp one night to look upon her sleeping lover. As Psyche bends to embrace him, a drop of hot oil falls from the lamp and wakens the radiant god, and the "epiphany" of Eros is suddenly concluded. As Eros vanishes, Psyche, like Lucius, understands the consequence of her foolish curiosity: separation from deity.

Impelled by her brief foretaste of divine bliss, Psyche begins a desperate search for her vanished consort. Her wanderings bring her to the temple of Venus, who is still angry that a mere mortal has been compared to her and angrier still that her son Eros has fallen in love with Psyche against her express command. In her wrath, Venus assigns impossible tasks for Psyche. With divine help, however, Psyche is able to complete these trials, including acquiring from Persephone, Queen of the Underworld, a bit of her beauty in a box. Overwhelmed once again by curiosity, Psyche peeks into the forbidden box only to be overcome by the deadly sleep of the underworld, which it also contains. Meanwhile, Eros, imprisoned by Venus for his transgression of her will, escapes and wakens Psyche from her deathlike sleep. Venus's objection to the unequal match is finally quelled when Jupiter gives Psyche the draught of immortality, and the couple is received into the company of the gods.

The story of Psyche and Eros appears on one level as a diverting tale told within the context of the fantastic adventures of Lucius; but on another level it encapsulates the structure of the entire novel.[5] On the one hand, the earthly experiences of Lucius are paralleled by the mythological experiences of Psyche: Lucius is a servant of Isis, Psyche is a servant of Venus. Lucius is transformed into an ass through his erotic curiosity; Psyche is separated from Eros because of her erotic curiosity. Both conditions of alienation result in wandering as Lucius seeks to regain his humanity and Psyche seeks reunion with her divine consort. In his wanderings Lucius serves many masters just as Psyche undergoes numerous trials. Lucius symbolically dies, and Psyche descends to the underworld. Both characters are saved from death,

Lucius through the grace of Isis and Psyche through the love of Eros. As Lucius enters the realm of the goddess through initiation, so Psyche is received into the community of the gods.

The wanderings of Psyche in search of Eros suggest, on the other hand, her identification with the goddess Isis, who wandered the world in search of her husband, Osiris. For the reader, the story of the wandering Psyche provides a clue to the wanderings of the eavesdropping ass and to his final salvation. Indeed, in the incident following this tale, the abducted girl to whom the story had been told is rescued by her bridegroom even as Psyche was rescued by hers. The earthly wanderings of Lucius, like those of Psyche, follow in the very footsteps of the goddess, not only in the final initiation but throughout life itself. As Isis was finally reunited with Osiris and Psyche with Eros, so Lucius will be reunited with the goddess—and with his own true nature.

What at first seemed a mere fairy tale told for diversion in the midst of Lucius's chaotic world is revealed, from the perspective of the novel's concluding Isiac epiphany, as a veiled Isis myth. This final episode not only culminates a collection of seemingly bizarre tales with its religious moral, but is also the key to an effective religious system that structures and is structured by the entire novel.

The Cosmic World of Apuleius

Like the religious novel of Apuleius, the astronomical compendium of Ptolemy, his contemporary, sums up its epoch. The Ptolemaic architecture of the cosmos structured and supported Hellenistic mythic formulations and was assumed by such writers as Apuleius.

With the Ptolemaic bifurcation of the cosmos into the sublunar terrestrial and the superlunar celestial realms, the Earth Mother of traditional geocentric mythology was transformed into the governing luminous principle of the night sky, the lunar Queen of Heaven. Lucius describes her dazzling power on the occasion of the full moon:

> About the first watch of the night, when as I had slept my first sleep, I awakened with sudden fear, and saw the moon shining bright as when she is at the full, and seemingly as though she leaped out of the sea. Then I thought with myself that this was the most secret time, when the goddess had most puissance and force, considering that all human things be governed by her providence; and that not

> only all beasts private and tame, wild and savage, be made strong by
> the governance of her light and godhead, but also things inanimate
> and without life; and I considered that all bodies in the heavens, the
> earth, and the seas be by her increasing motions increased, and by
> her diminishing motions diminished.   *Met.* XI, 1

When the chthonic goddess was transposed from her terrestrial
locus within the traditional world image to the lunar realm of the
Ptolemaic cosmic image, she was no longer viewed as a dependable
source of nurture. Inconstant as the moon itself, she became a capricious goddess who subjugated even the powerful Olympians to her
now universal rule and who withheld her favors at will.[6]

A feminine principle of cosmic rule was derived from the qualita-
tive theory of physical reality formulated by Aristotle and was generally accepted, with modifications, throughout the Hellenistic period.[7]
Aristotle postulated that material reality is constituted by four elements: earth, air, fire, and water. These four elements in turn are
constituted by a combination of two of the four primary qualities:
cold, dry, hot, and moist. Thus, fire is the combination of hot and
dry, air is the combination of hot and moist, water is the combination
of cold and moist, and earth is the combination of cold and dry. On
this basis, Aristotle was able to explain material change in general by
assuming the changing proportions of qualities in which each could be
replaced by its opposite.[8]

One principle of opposition, that of male-female, was already
grounded in pre-Socratic thought.[9] Aristotle followed Empedocles,
for example, in associating the masculine principle with the quality of
heat and the feminine principle with the quality of cold.[10] Consequently, Ptolemy was reporting conventional wisdom when he wrote
of

> two primary kinds of natures, male and female, and of the forces
> already mentioned that of the moist is especially feminine—for as a
> general thing this element is present to a great degree in all females,
> and the other rather in males.

Thus, he continues,

> the moon and Venus are feminine, because they share most largely
> in the moist, . . . the sun, Saturn, Jupiter, and Mars are masculine,
> and Mercury [is] common to both genders, inasmuch as he produces
> the dry and the moist alike.   *Tet.* I, 6

Day "is more masculine because of its heat . . . and night more feminine because of its moisture" (*Tet.* I, 7). Finally, the sun's power "is found to be heating and, to a certain degree, drying," whereas "the moon's power consists of humidifying, clearly because it is close to the earth" (*Tet.* I, 4). Thus, the sublunar realm generally, including the planets Earth and Moon, is composed primarily of the elements earth and water, is characterized by the qualities of dry and moist coldness, and is therefore accorded feminine attributes.

In mythic correspondence to the Ptolemaic revolution, a drama of antitheses is played out in the cosmic arena between a feminine principle of randomness in nature and the lunar goddess, the feminine principle of celestial order. The mythological departure of the sacred from the terrestrial into the lunar realm paralleled the breakdown of local autonomy in the Hellenistic sociopolitical arena in the face of imperial internationalism. With this celestial consolidation of the divine guarantors of cosmic order, terrestrial existence remained under the control of chance.

The Mythic World of Apuleius

Fortune

The opening story of *The Golden Ass* foreshadows the fortuitous plight of Lucius and suggests the fortuitousness of Hellenistic existence as a whole. In this tale Aristomenes, a chance companion of Lucius, tells him of his own chance meeting with a long-lost friend, Socrates, who had come into some bad luck and had become a beggar. Attacked by bandits while on a business trip to Macedonia, Socrates finally escapes to an inn, only to fall under the power of a wicked sorceress, Meroe. Ultimately, however, Socrates does not blame Meroe for his present condition; rather, he blames Fortune and warns Aristomenes:

> O my friend . . . , now perceive I well that you are ignorant of the whirling changes, the unstable forces, and slippery inconstancy of fortune. *Met.* I, 6

By the end of this opening tale, Fortune has placed Aristomenes in a situation of ill-fortune similar to that of Socrates, and before long, Lucius too will know the effects of Fortune's buffetings.

A personified Fortune was widely worshipped by the third century B.C.E. and possessed temples in nearly all the great Greek cities.[11] Pliny, writing in the first century C.E., described her universal rule:

> Everywhere in the whole world at every hour by all men's voices Fortune alone is invoked and named . . . and we are so much at the mercy of chance that Chance herself, by whom God is proved uncertain, takes the place of God. *HN* II, 5, 22

The universal recognition of Fortune's effects is often viewed as the final stage in the secularization of Hellenistic religion, in which, as Pliny notes, the personification of the unpredictable and the unexplained "takes the place of God."[12] But she has also been described as the most important deity of the Hellenistic era because of her universal sovereignity over mortals and immortals alike.[13]

Fortune (in Greek, *tychē;* in Latin, *fortuna*) means chance or luck, both good and ill. Embodied in a single image, the goddess' ambiguity or capriciousness, her double nature, positive and negative, is her most characteristic trait.[14] In the words of Pliny:

> [Fortune is] alone accused, alone impeached, alone pondered, alone applauded, alone rebuked and visited with reproaches; deemed volatile and indeed by most men blind as well, wayward, inconstant, uncertain, fickle in her favours and favouring the unworthy. To her is debited all that is spent and credited all that is received, she alone fills both pages in the whole of mortals' account. *HN* II, 5, 22

This double significance of Tyche/Fortuna is mirrored in the intricate and overlapping relations among the characters who inhabit the seemingly thinly connected adventures of Lucius. It structures the overall story and orders even the most chaotic of its situations.

Consequently, Lucius is not only subject to the buffetings of ill fortune, but is also the recipient of the aid of Isis, the beneficent "fortune that is not blind, but can see" (*Met.* XI, 15). This sympathetic aspect of Isis was known also as *Agathē Tychē* (Good Fortune), a virtue commonly attributed to her.[15]

The rule of Tyche/Fortuna constitutes a coherent structure by which Apuleius organized his novel and which organizes the historical confusion highlighted by the situation of Hellenistic religious syncretism portrayed in the novel. The sovereignty of Tyche/Fortuna was imaged by antithetical feminine personifications and attributes and ordered by a process of transformation in which only the sympathetic aspect of this feminine structure could overcome the ambiguous or antipathetic aspect of the same feminine structure. This mytho-cosmological dynamic of antipathetic/sympathetic feminine ambiguity gave structure to religious formations throughout the entire Hellenistic period and directed its syncretistic dynamic. As summarized mythologically by the priest of Isis in Apuleius's novel:

> O my friend Lucius, after the endurance of so many labours and the escape of so many tempests of fortune, thou art now at length come to the port and haven of rest and mercy. Neither did thy noble lineage, thy dignity, neither thy excellent doctrine anything avail thee; but because thou didst turn to servile pleasures, by a little folly of thy youthfulness, thou hast had a sinister reward of thy unprosperous curiosity. But howsoever the blindness of fortune tormented thee in divers dangers, so it is that now by her unthoughtful malice thou art come to this present felicity of religion. Let fortune go and fume with fury in another place; let her find some other matter to execute her cruelty; for fortune hath no puissance against them which have devoted their lives to serve and honour the majesty of our goddess. . . . Know thou that now thou art safe, and under the protection of that fortune that is not blind but can see, who by her clear light doth lighten the other gods: wherefore rejoice, and take a convenable countenance to thy white habit, and follow with joyful steps the pomp of this devout and honourable procession; let such, which be not devout to the goddess, see and acknowledge their error. 'Behold, here is Lucius that is delivered from his former so great miseries by the providence of the goddess Isis, and rejoiceth therefore and triumpheth of victory over his fortune.'
>
> *Met.* XI, 15

Wandering

The transformation of existence from the social conventions of the polis to a newly articulated individualism, far from being the symbol of possibility and freedom it became for Renaissance Europe, was understood in the Hellenistic world as a problematic, Lucian-like wandering in a greatly expanded world moved by larger forces over which one had no control and of which one had little understanding. Buffeted by the caprice of Fortune, the quest of the dubious hero, Lucius, for the antidotal rose is haphazard. In contrast to the directed nature of traditional heroic quests, the governing metaphor for habitation in the Hellenistic world became aimless wandering. Hellenistic existence had been propelled into an individualism without instruction, an aimlessness motivated by a profound sense of alienation;[16] in short, into a "crisis of freedom."[17]

The Hellenistic problem of individualism is imaginatively portrayed in Apuleius's novel by the transformation of Lucius into the wandering ass. In the Egyptian Isis-Osiris myth, the ass was the theriomorphic or animal form of Set (known to the Greeks as Typhon), the dark twin brother of Isis and Osiris, and their antagonist. Thus, the asinine Lucius embodied all that was opposite and abhorrent to the goddess Isis and publically represented everything that was contrary to the religious life.[18] As the ancient personification of the arid Egyptian desert—in opposition to the fertility of the Nile, which was associated with Osiris, and the fecund earth of the irrigated banks, associated with Isis—Typhon the ass signified death in the face of life. Lucius's ill fortune was nothing less than a ritual death, narratively elaborated. The rose that could transform him and that represents completion, perfection, and regeneration was the emblem of Venus, with whom the savior goddess Isis identified herself, according to Apuleius, in her final epiphany to Lucius.[19]

Salvation

Throughout his wanderings Lucius is unable to discover any ordering principle in his world apart from the savior, Isis. Savior (in Greek, *sōtēr* [masc.]; *sōteira* [fem.]) means deliverer, preserver, protector, or healer, and was an appellation of both gods and humans, male and female. Saviors in the Greek and Hellenistic world included not only deities such as Zeus, Heracles, Asclepius, Isis, Tyche, and Jesus, but also famous mortals such as Epicurus, Alexander, Ptolemy of Egypt, and the Roman emperors. The Greek title "savior" thus designated extraordinary personalities, divine or human, who were active in world affairs and who were considered to have transformed a situation for the better, whether militarily, politically, intellectually, or religiously. Salvation meant transformation. In the fictive world of Apuleius, only Isis, the feminine as savior, is able to offer an alternative to Tyche/Fortuna, the feminine as capricious; only the terrestrial feminine principle restructured as the soteriological "Queen of Heaven" is victorious over "cruel Fortune"; only the savior goddess can effect a transformation of existence by offering a religious alternative to a dangerous and chaotic world.

In contrast to the classical Greek view of fate (*moira*), the differentiation of a positive and negative Tyche/Fortuna entails a more ethical concept. Value judgments are not generally attributed to the personified *Moirai* but only to their effects. Whereas one could not escape either the positive or negative effects of *moira,* one might be saved from domination by a negative Tyche/Fortuna through sympathetic identity with her positive side.

The Social World of Apuleius

Home

An ancient Greek proverb states:

> It is better to be at home:
> harm may come out of doors.
> *Hymn Hom. Herm.* IV, 36–37

The great myths of Western civilization contain epic cycles in which the hero, after completion of his heroic tasks, must find his way home again. His successful homecoming is the final heroic task. We find this theme in the quest for immortality of the Mesopotamian King Gilgamesh and his return home to mortality in Urak; in the collective exodus of the fledgling nation Israel from slavery in Egypt to its home in the promised land; and in the Hellenic journey of Odysseus, who returns to Ithaca following the Trojan War. Lucius, however, rejected his "home life" for a life of sensuality and magic,[20] and his troubles befell him while he was away from home. As Fotis warned Lucius:

> there is a rabble of well-born youth that disturbeth the public peace, and you may see many murdered about in the streets, neither can the armies of the governor, for that they are afar off, rid the city of this great plague. *Met.* II, 18

In the ancient world one's home provided a sanctuary against such ne'er-do-wells and marauding robbers, as well as wild animals and other more mysterious powers.

To provide protection from external malevolent forces, houses in the ancient world were constructed like fortresses. Generally, town houses were built with a series of rooms around a central courtyard upon which all windows opened. One entered from the street into this central courtyard through a well-fortified gate. A country house was similarly constructed except that it was surrounded by a protecting wall or fence. Such houses provided safe retreat from external harm.[21]

Located in the center of these homes was the hearth (in Greek, *hestia,* meaning also "home" or "family"). The *hestia* provided warmth and nourishment within the protective bounds of the house and was the center of family piety. The transfer of fire from the family hearth to each newly established home represented and ensured familial continuity. When families came together in a village or town, a public hearth, located in the center of the council house, was lit by fires from the hearths of member families. And when any new Greek colony was founded, the emigrants carried fire from the hearth of the founding state to kindle that of the new city.[22]

Consistent with the traditional Greek view of sacrality, the sanctity of the hearth was not conferred but was considered immanent, as belonging to its nature. These hearths were presided over by a goddess also named Hestia (in Latin, Vestia), the first child of Cronos and Rhea. Hestia, consequently, was the guardian not only of home and family but also of the town and later of the city states; she was always invoked at state offerings and festivals.[23] The hearth as sacred center extended from every family to the state, to any collection or federation of states, and, through Hestia, to the hearth of the gods, the cosmic center. Home, then, was not simply a shelter offering protection from alien forces, but a metaphor for existence in harmony with cosmic order, a secure and meaningful existence in which "it is better to be."

In contrast to the traditional social organization around home and family, Hellenization entailed urbanization. Plutarch's report that Alexander himself founded seventy cities (*De Alex. Fort.*1) is an exaggeration. Nevertheless, he did found a good number of cities, and Plutarch's estimate emphasizes the relationship of citification and Alexander's vision of cosmopolitan civilization.

The list of new Greek cities includes native cities refounded with a Greek constitution and name, military colonies, and trade centers, in addition to actual newly founded cities, of which Alexandria is the most famous. Each city included its surrounding territory or *chōra,* upon which it depended for food. It has been estimated that each resident of a city required ten inhabitants of the countryside to ensure his or her support.[24] Shunning the segregation of space as seen in traditional house architecture, Hellenistic urban planning strove for an interconnecting network of buildings, primarily by means of the construction of *stoa* or roofed colonnades. With its *gymnasium* and theatre, the Hellenistic city was the center of Greek economy, language, education, and culture for the Hellenistic world.

Magic

Away from home, magical powers threatened, and to read Apuleius's *The Golden Ass* is to enter this magical world.[25] In the opening tale Aristomenes, whom Lucius encountered on his way to Thessaly, the land of sorceresses, tells Lucius of Socrates' fear of the Thessalian witch Meroe, who is able

> to bring down the sky, to bear up the earth, to turn the water into hills and the hills into running waters, to call up the terrestrial spirits into the air, and to pull the gods out of the heavens, to extinguish the planets, and to lighten the very darkness of hell.   *Met.* I, 8

Pamphile, the wife of Lucius's host in Hypata, was also a sorceress. She was able, like Homer's Circe (*Od.* 10, 203–247), to transform anyone who displeased her into "stone, sheep, or some other beast." And Fotis, Pamphile's servant girl, was instructed in "all the magical formulas" of her mistress. Although Lucius's host, Milo, had extended his hospitality to Lucius, Lucius was not at home in this foreign region of Thessaly with its strange practices and customs. His troubles began when he meddled in the magical nature of this world.

Like a character from his own novel, Apuleius himself had been formally accused of winning an attractive and wealthy wife by magic. His defense against this charge, the *Apologia,* provides another glimpse into Hellenistic magic.[26]

Derived from the ancient chthonic cults of the earth goddess,[27] Hellenistic magic included a multitude of practices.[28] Apuleius divided these practices into good and evil (*Apol.* 9, 42, 61, 63), the evil ones being those which bring injury to someone.[29] Apuleius further divided good magic into popular and philosophical magic. Popular magic involved power over the order of nature, so that, as Apuleius writes in *The Golden Ass,*

the swift rivers might be forced to run against their courses; the sea
to be bound immovable; the winds to lose their force and die; the
sun to be restrained from his natural journey; the moon to drop her
foam upon the earth; the stars to be pulled down from heaven; the
day to be darkened; and the night to be made to continue for ever.

Met. I, 3

There is, however, a "magic" associated with the philosophical investigation of the universe as well. According to Apuleius, such philosophers as Anaxagoras, Leucippus, Democritus, Epicurus, and Pythagoras had been called magicians because they "explore the origins and
elements of material things" (*Apol.* 27, 31).

All magical practice and investigation assumed a finite cosmos in
which all things are related to one another through a cosmic sympathy
(in Greek, *sympatheia*). As Plotinus, the third-century c.e. Neo-
platonist, reflected:

But how do magic spells work? By sympathy and by the fact that
there is a natural concord of things that are alike and opposition of
things that are different, and by the rich variety of the many powers
which go to make up the life of the one living creature.

Enn. IV, 4, 40

A cosmic harmony, therefore, describes a system of sympathetic and
antipathetic natural forces.[30] These forces of nature, which could be
personified as demons, described a relation assumed to exist between
all things within the finite cosmos, especially between an internal
nature, whether of man, home, temple, or city, and all that was
external to it; between the microcosm, the "small world" of human
activity, and the macrocosm, the "large world" of external reality. An
example of this cosmic relationship is found in the writings of the
first-century c.e. Jewish philosopher Philo. In his account of the Babylonians, he writes:

They have set up a harmony between things on earth and things on
high, between heavenly things and earthly. Following as it were the
laws of musical proportion, they have exhibited the universe as a
perfect concord or symphony produced by a sympathetic affinity
between its parts, separated indeed in space, but housemates in
kinship.   *Mig.* 178

Magic was the set of practices that assumed, in common with religion and science,[31] a cosmic system of thought and knowledge—and thereby, of the forces of nature—and which consequently could effect sympathetic rapport with these forces.[32] This magical "way of looking at the world"[33] provided an alternative to the terrestrial disorder personified as Tyche/Fortuna. It established relations, both sympathetically and antipathetically, between its practitioners and others (mortals, gods, and the physical world) by expressing or objectifying the cosmos as an orderly and harmonious whole, and by establishing thereby their at-homeness in the world.[34]

A Hellenistic resurgence of interest in magic was first challenged by nascent Christianity (Acts 19:18–20) and then by imperial Rome, which feared its power.[35] The concerted opposition of Christian Rome finally suppressed its public practice by the end of the Hellenistic era in the fourth century C.E.[36]

The World of Lucius

The world of Apuleius's Lucius was a system in transformation. Alexander's empire had transformed the world from parochialism to internationalism, from a collection of autonomous and self-sufficient city-states to an interdependent but competitive and bounded empire, from a defined social reality to a problematic individualism. Concurrently, a new architecture of the world was objectified by the Ptolemaic revolution, which structured a sympathetic order articulated as the rule of Agathe Tyche, who was mythologized as the providential goddess and related to by magico-religious practices. Just as the protective, walled home, the actual and metaphorical place in which "it is better to be," defended against the wilderness, and the battlements of cities and borders of empire challenged the ambitions of "barbarians," so the hierarchical enclosures of the cosmos protected from external chaos. In terms of the sympathetic principle of microcosmic-macrocosmic parallelism, to be safe at home was simultaneously to be secure in the world and protected from its antithetic powers.

Apuleius's novel portrays life in this ambiguous world as an aimless wandering among the alternatives of existence that flourished in the midst of these social, political, cosmic, and mythic transformations. It portrays, too, the Hellenistic mythic, magical, and mystery relations to the capricious rule of Tyche/Fortuna and serves well as an introduction to the labyrinth of Hellenistic syncretism.

Notes

1. The translation cited is W. Adlington's sixteenth-century translation, revised by S. Gaselee and published as part of the Loeb Classical Library series (Cambridge, Mass.: Harvard University Press, 1915).

2. Jack Lindsay (trans.), *The Golden Ass* (Bloomington, Ind.: Indiana University Press, 1962), p. 28.

3. P. G. Walsh, *The Roman Novel: The Satyricon of Petronius and the Metamorphoses of Apuleius* (Cambridge: Cambridge University Press, 1970), p. 186; James Tatum, *Apuleius and "The Golden Ass"* (Ithaca, N.Y.: Cornell University Press, 1979), pp. 101–104; Helmut Koester, *Introduction to the New Testament,* vol. I: *History, Culture and Religion of the Hellenistic Age,* Eng. trans. (Philadelphia: Fortress, 1982; Berlin and New York: Walter de Gruyter, 1982), pp. 136–140.

4. A. D. Nock, *Conversion: The Old and the New in Religion from Alexander the Great to Augustine of Hippo* (Oxford: Oxford University Press, 1961), p. 138. Nock concludes that *The Golden Ass* represents "the high-water mark of piety which grew out of the mystery religions." See also Reinhold Merkelbach, *Roman und Mysterium in der Antike* (Munich and Berlin: C. H. Beck, 1962), pp. 1–90, 333–340.

5. The following interpretation of the Psyche and Eros story follows that of Merkelbach, pp. 1–53.

6. H. R. Patch concludes that Fortuna under the Roman Empire "is in control of the universe, but she is quite arbitrary about it." See "The Tradition of the Goddess Fortuna in Roman Literature and in the Transitional Period," *Smith College Studies in Modern Language,* 3 (1922), pp. 132–177: 147.

7. Samuel Sambursky, *The Physical World of Late Antiquity* (New York: Basic Books, 1962), p. 35.

8. Sambursky, pp. 34–35.

9. G. E. R. Lloyd, *Polarity and Analogy: Two Types of Argumentation in Early Greek Thought* (Cambridge: Cambridge University Press, 1966), p. 16.

10. Lloyd, pp. 17, 59; see Empedocles, Fragments 65 and 67, in Kathleen Freeman, *Ancilla to the Pre-Socratic Philosophers* (Cambridge: Mass.: Harvard University Press, 1983), p. 59.

11. Percey Gardner, *New Chapters in Greek Art* (New York: AMS Press, 1971), pp. 257–268.

12. Martin Nilsson, *Geschichte der Griechischen Religion,* 2nd ed., vol. II (Munich: C. H. Beck, 1961), p. 202.

13. See, for example, Franz Cumont, *Astrology and Religion Among the Greeks and Romans,* trans. J. B. Baker (New York: Dover, 1960), p. 89: "Thus belief in Fate not only (1) became a source of moral inspiration of noble minds, but also (2) provided a justification of the necessity of positive worship."

14. See Iiro Kajanto, "Fortuna," *Aufstieg und Niedergang der Römischen Welt* II, 17. 1 (Berlin and New York: Walter de Gruyter, 1981), pp. 502–588. Kajanto distinguishes between the fickle *tychē/fortuna* and the positive Latin *fortuna,* pp. 525–532.

15. Vera Frederika Vanderlip, *The Four Greek Hymns of Isidorus and the Cult of Isis,* American Studies in Papyrology 12 (Toronto: A. M. Hakkert, 1972), pp. 31–32, 95–96.

16. E. R. Dodds, *Pagan and Christian in an Age of Anxiety* (New York: Norton, 1970).

17. Peter Brown, "The Rise and Function of the Holy Man in Late Antiquity," in *Society and the Holy in Late Antiquity* (Berkeley, Calif.: University of California Press, 1982), p. 148.

18. Reinhold Merkelbach, pp. 1–2.

19. J. Gwyn Griffiths, *Apuleius of Madauros: The Isis-Book* (*Metamorphoses, Book XI*) (Leiden: E. J. Brill, 1975), pp. 159–161.

20. Sharon Kelly Heyob, *The Cult of Isis Among Women in the Graeco-Roman World* (Leiden: E. J. Brill, 1975), p. 68.

21. Martin P. Nilsson, *Greek Folk Religion* (New York: Harper, 1961), pp. 65–67.

22. Nilsson, pp. 72–76; A. J. Graham, *Colony and Mother City in Ancient Greece,* rev. ed. (Chicago: Ares, 1984), p. 25.

23. Walter Burkert, *Greek Religion,* trans. John Raffan (Cambridge, Mass.: Harvard University Press, 1985), p. 61.

24. G. E. M. de Ste. Croix, *The Class Struggle in the Ancient Greek World* (Ithaca, N.Y.: Cornell University Press, 1981), pp. 10–11.

25. Howard Clark Kee, *Miracle in the Early Christian World* (New Haven, Conn.: Yale University Press, 1983), pp. 136–138.

26. H. E. Butler (trans.), *The Apologia and Florida of Apuleius of Madaura* (Westport, Conn.: Greenwood Press, 1970).

27. Georg Luck, *Arcana Mundi: Magic and Occult in the Greek and Roman Worlds* (Baltimore: Johns Hopkins University Press, 1985), p. 5.

28. John M. Hull, *Hellenistic Magic and the Synoptic Tradition,* Studies in Biblical Theology, series 2, no. 28 (Naperville, Ill.: SCM Press, 1974), chap. III; Morton Smith, *Jesus the Magician* (San Francisco: Harper & Row, 1978), chap. 6.

29. Lynn Thorndike, *A History of Magic and Experimental Science,* vol. 1 (New York: Columbia University Press, 1964), p. 235.

30. Hull, pp. 41–42; Luck, p. 8.

31. Allan, F. Segal, "Hellenistic Magic: Some Questions of Definition," in R. van den Broek and M. J. Vermaseren (eds.), *Studies in Gnosticism and Hellenistic Religions* (Leiden: E. J. Brill, 1981), pp. 349–350.

32. K. F. Smith, "Magic (Greek and Roman)," in James Hastings (ed.), *Encyclopedia of Religion and Ethics,* vol. 8 (New York: Charles Scribner's Sons, 1916), p. 281.

33. Thorndike, p. 4.
34. Luck, p. 44; Hans Dieter Betz (ed. and trans.), *The Greek Magical Papyri* (Chicago: University of Chicago Press, 1986), p. xlvii.
35. Luck, p. 14; Betz, p. xli.
36. Luck, p. 46.

Selected Bibliography

Translations of Apuleius's Metamorphoses

Apuleius, *The Golden Ass,* trans. S. Gaselee, in the Loeb Classical Library (Cambridge, Mass.: Harvard University Press, 1915), is a revised version of W. Adlington's sixteenth-century translation, which attempts to preserve in English the exuberant and intentionally archaized Latin employed by Apuleius.

Robert Graves, *The Transformations of Lucius, Otherwise Known as "The Golden Ass"* (New York: Noonday Press, 1967), is a paraphrastic but highly readable translation.

Jack Lindsay (trans.), *The Golden Ass* (Bloomington, Ind.: Indiana University Press, 1962).

Commentaries on Apuleius's Metamorphoses

J. Gwyn Griffiths, *Apuleius of Madauros: The Isis-Book (Metamorphoses, Book XI)* (Leiden: E. J. Brill, 1975).

R. T. van der Paardt, *Apuleius Madaurensis, The Metamorphoses: A Commentary on Book III with Text and Introduction* (Amsterdam: A. M. Hakkert, 1971).

James Tatum, *Apuleius and The Golden Ass* (Ithaca, N.Y.: Cornell University Press, 1979).

Studies of Apuleius's Metamorphoses

A.-J. Festugière, *Personal Religion Among the Greeks* (Berkeley, Calif.: University of California Press, 1954), chap. V.

Reinhold Merkelbach, *Roman und Mysterium in der Antike* (Munich and Berlin: C. H. Beck, 1962).

A. D. Nock, *Conversion: The Old and the New in Religion from Alexander the Great to Augustine of Hippo* (Oxford: Oxford University Press, 1961), chap. IX.

Greco-Roman Houses

Bertha C. Rider, *Ancient Greek Houses* (Chicago: Argonaut, 1964).

Magic

Hans Dieter Betz (ed. and trans.), *The Greek Magical Papyri* (Chicago: University of Chicago Press, 1986).

A.-J. Festugière, *La Révélation d'Hermès Trismégiste,* vol. 1 (Paris: J. Gabalda, 1944–1954).

John M. Hull, *Hellenistic Magic and the Synoptic Tradition,* Studies in Biblical Theology, series 2, no. 28 (Naperville, Ill.: SCM Press, 1974).

G. E. R. Lloyd, *Magic, Reason and Experience: Studies in the Origins and Development of Greek Science* (Cambridge: Cambridge University Press, 1979).

Georg Luck, *Arcana Mundi: Magic and Occult in the Greek and Roman Worlds* (Baltimore: Johns Hopkins University Press, 1985).

Allan F. Segal, "Hellenistic Magic: Some Questions of Definition" in R. van den Broek and M. J. Vermaseren (eds.), *Studies in Gnosticism and Hellenistic Religions* (Leiden: E. J. Brill, 1981).

K. F. Smith, "Magic (Greek and Roman)," in James Hastings (ed.), *Encyclopedia of Religion and Ethics,* vol. 8 (New York: Charles Scribner's Sons, 1916).

Lynn Thorndike, *A History of Magic and Experimental Science,* vol. 1 (New York: Columbia University Press, 1964).

Deity as Savior

S. G. F. Brandon (ed.), *The Saviour God* (Manchester: Manchester University Press, 1963).

Fortuna

Iiro Kajanto, "Fortuna," *Aufstieg und Niedergang der Römischen Welt* II, 17. 1 (Berlin and New York: Walter de Gruyter, 1981), pp. 502–558.

H. R. Patch, *The Tradition of the Goddess Fortuna,* Smith College Studies in Modern Language, 3 (1922), pp. 132–177, is the classic study.

Cosmology

F. C. Burkitt, *Church and Gnosis* (Cambridge: Cambridge University Press, 1932).

E. R. Dodds, *Pagan and Christian in an Age of Anxiety* (New York: Norton, 1970).

J. L. E. Dreyer, *A History of Astronomy from Thales to Kepler* (New York: Dover, 1953).

Robert Eisler, *Weltenmantel und Himmelzeit: Religionsgeschichtliche Untersuchungen zur Urgeschichte des antiken Weltbildes* (Munich: C. H. Beck, 1910).

Mircea Eliade, *The Myth of the Eternal Return: Cosmos and History,* trans. Willard R. Trask (Princeton, N.J.: Princeton University Press, 1954), is the classic history of religions study.

A.-J. Festugière, "Cadre de la mystique hellénistique," in *Aux Sources de la Tradition Chrétienne, Mélanges offerts à Maurice Goguel,* Bibliothèque Théologique (Neuchatel and Paris: Delachaux and Niestlé, 1950), offers an important overview.

Charles H. Kahn, *Anaximander and the Origins of Greek Cosmology* (Philadelphia: Centrum Philadelphia, 1985).

Milton K. Munitz (ed.), *Theories of the Universe from Babylonian Myth to Modern Science* (New York: Free Press, 1957).

Martin P. Nilsson, *Greek Piety,* trans. H. J. Rose (New York: Norton, 1969), pp. 96–103.

Samuel Sambursky, *The Physical World of Late Antiquity* (New York: Basic Books, 1962).

Hans-Friedrich Weiss, *Untersuchung zur Kosmologie des hellenistischen und palästinischen Judentums* (Berlin: Akademie-Verlag, 1966).

2

Hellenistic Piety

With the emergence of Hellenistic culture, the practices that characterized traditional Greek piety were neither abandoned nor significantly changed[1] but continued alongside the emerging Hellenistic
patterns of religion as an underlying stratum, a generative context.
There was thus little that was intrinsically "Hellenistic" about the
piety of the Hellenistic folk. Relying on an assumed natural order of
things, piety adapted formulations of an earlier system to counter the
Hellenistic rule of Tyche/Fortuna. The Hellenistic conventions of folk
piety belonged, therefore, to the same world as the so-called "higher"
forms of spirituality and knowledge associated with the Hellenistic
mysteries and with gnosis. And perhaps more than the Mysteries and
gnosis, the practices of Hellenistic folk piety manifested the patterns
of the world within which they had meaning. Before turning our
attention to the mystery and gnostic traditions, therefore, we must
spend some time among these folk, for it is to them that the "higher"
expressions of religiosity appealed and from whom they attracted
their initiates.

Traditional Piety

Piety consists of those everyday practices which maintain domestic
and social order. As an example, the Greeks would place a little food

on the hearth before a meal, most likely as an offering to Hestia, goddess of the hearth, and would pour a little wine on the floor in offering to the guardian of the house.[2] Such honor or respect for home and family, of course, also extended to and embraced the polis or state.[3]

Although Hellenization was primarily an urban phenomenon, most of the population did not inhabit such intellectual and cultural centers as Athens and Alexandria, but rather were rural folk pursuing an agrarian way of life. In the traditional world, agriculture was tied to a deep appreciation of and profound respect for the land and nature. Yet the Mother Goddesses, who personified agrarian piety, were fickle. They presided over both life and death, plenty and famine, success and failure, and so became known as Tyche, or chance. Such Greek festivals as the *thesmophoria,* or fall planting festival; the *thargēlia,* or pre-harvest festival of purification; and the *thalysia,* or spring harvest festival, gave calendrical order to seasonal change.[4]

Traditional practices associated with the piety of family and field assumed a localized order of things that oriented and structured a secure existence. With the Ptolemaic revolution, the loci of this order became removed from their regional distribution and were universalized. The problem addressed by Hellenistic piety was not the absence of an order of things, but access to it.

Hellenistic Philosophy and the Rational Order of Things

Although Hellenistic philosophy is beyond the scope of this survey, it is briefly mentioned here to suggest the assumptions it shared with piety. Both dealt with the existential problems of the newly constellating Hellenistic world in similar ways.[5]

Philosophy in the Hellenistic World

There was an intellectual counterpart to the social, political, and cosmological transformations that characterized the Hellenistic age. The great age of Greek classical philosophy concluded with the death of Aristotle in 322 B.C.E., one year after the death of his student Alexander the Great. The cosmological and metaphysical speculations of the classical age gave way to more immediate ethical concerns: how does one conduct oneself as an individual under the transitory conditions of the Hellenistic world in a situation of homelessness, in a hostile world buffeted by fortune? This problem was summarized toward the end of the age by Plotinus, the third-century C.E. founder of Neoplatonism:

> All things are indicated [by the stars] and all things happen according to causes, but there are two kinds of these; and some happenings are brought about by the soul, others through other causes, those round about it. And souls, in all that they do, when they do it according to right reason, act of themselves, whenever they do act, but in everything else are hindered in their own action and are passive rather than active. So other things [not the soul] are responsible for not thinking; and it is perhaps correct to say that the soul acts unthinkingly according to destiny, at least for people who think that destiny is an external cause; but the best actions come from ourselves.   *Enn.* III, 1, 10

With piety, philosophy assumed a finite ordered world that existed in the face of an apparent arbitrariness, and a knowledge of that order which was available directly to rational inquiry.

Hellenistic philosophy countered Tyche/Fortuna with its rational knowledge. The teachings of Epicurus (circa 341–270 B.C.E.) and of his contemporary, Zeno (335–263 B.C.E.), the founder of Stoicism, exemplify the philosophical response.

The Epicureans

The Epicureans withdrew from the fortuitous world by cultivating a reflective and prudent life of the mind. In appropriating the atomic theory of the fifth-century B.C.E. philosopher Democritus, they understood the world materially. They believed that the totality of the cosmos, including the body and the soul, was a wholly natural combination resulting from an infinite supply of atoms that at some point would disperse. The Epicureans did not deny the existence of the gods, who provided a model for man, but they rejected any possibility of the gods' intervention in the affairs of this world. They followed Epicurus in challenging any view of existence determined by Fortune:

> Who, then, is superior in thy judgement to such a [hedonistic] man?
> He holds a holy belief concerning the gods, and is altogether free from the fear of death. He has diligently considered the end fixed by

nature. . . . Destiny, which some introduce as sovereign over all things, he laughs to scorn, affirming rather that some things happen of necessity, others by chance, others through our own agency. For he sees that necessity destroys responsibility and that chance or fortune is inconstant; whereas our own actions are free, and it is to them that praise and blame naturally attach. It were better, indeed, to accept the legends of the gods than to bow beneath the yoke of destiny which natural philosophers have imposed. The one holds out some faint hope that we may escape if we honour the gods, while the necessity of the naturalists is deaf to all entreaties. Nor does he hold chance to be a god, as the world in general does, for in the acts of a god there is no disorder; nor to be a cause, though an uncertain one, for he believes that no good or evil is dispensed by chance to men so as to make life blessed, though it supplies the starting-point of great good and great evil. He believes that the misfortune of the wise is better than the prosperity of the fool. It is better, in short, that what is well judged in action should not owe its successful issues to the aid of chance.

Epicurus, *Ep. Men.* (*Diog. Laert.* X, 133–135)

Certainty in the face of chance is based upon the incontestability of one's immediate corporeal experience, which is free from any external divine or fortuitous control and consequently is accessible to rational inquiry. The Epicureans sought to experience pleasure to offset the ambiguities of fortune and to avoid disturbance and pain. "We do not mean the pleasures of the prodigal or the pleasures of sensuality, as we are understood to do by some through ignorance, prejudice, or wilful misrepresentation," Epicurus writes.

By pleasure we mean the absence of pain in the body and of trouble in the soul. . . . It is sober reasoning, searching out the grounds of every choice and avoidance, and banishing those beliefs through which the great tumults take possession of the soul.

Epicurus, *Ep. Men.* (*Diog. Laert.* X, 131)

Epicurean pleasure was in the intellectual pursuit of wisdom rather than in hedonistic activities, as convention later held.[6]

The Stoics

While the Epicureans sought to withdraw from a fortuitous world to the certainties of corporeal experience, the Stoics attempted to conform individual and political existence to the orderly cosmos they assumed it to be. Founded on the thought of Zeno, who had taught in one of the colonnades (in Greek, *stoa*) of Athens, Stoicism owed its popular success primarily to its ability to turn the various expressions of the "many-named" cosmic law into allegories of its own unitary philosophic principle. The Stoics' view of order was based on their assumption of one great law of nature that governed the totality of the cosmos, whether that law was imaged as the central fire, first evoked by the fifth-century B.C.E. philosopher Heraclitus, or whether known philosophically as a rational order of things (*logos*), cosmologically as the order of nature (*heimarmenē*), or theologically as the god Zeus. As expressed mythologically by Zeno's successor, Cleanthes (331–232 B.C.E.), in his "Hymn to Zeus":

> Most glorious of immortals, Zeus
> The many-named, almighty evermore,
> Nature's great Sovereign, ruling all by law
>
> • • •
>
> For thee this whole vast cosmos, wheeling round
> The earth, obeys, and where thou leadest
> It follows, ruled willingly by thee.
> *Hymn to Zeus*[7]

Thus, from a religious perspective the Stoics were pantheists: everything was derived from and participated in the First Principle. The Stoic philosophical goal was to live in harmony with this universal law of nature. To act in accordance with this law was to be free from the capriciousness of chance and to be at home in the world. As summarized by the first-century C.E. Stoic philosopher Seneca:

> Philosophy . . . moulds and constructs the soul; it orders our life, guides our conduct, shows us what we should do and what we should leave undone; it sits at the helm and directs our course as we waver amid uncertainties. Without it, no one can live fearlessly or in peace of mind. . . . We must be philosophers; whether Fate bind us down by an inexorable law, or whether God as arbiter of the universe has arranged everything, or whether Chance drives and tosses human affairs without method, philosophy ought to be our defence. She will encourage us to obey God cheerfully, but Fortune defiantly; she will teach us to follow God and endure Chance.
> *Ep.* XVI, 5–6

The Stoics provided a philosophical argument for knowing and accepting the rule of fate, and thereby a philosophical justification for pietistic practice.[8]

Philosophy and Piety

The various philosophies of this period were not sharply different from contemporary pietistic options insofar as both assumed a sympathetic order of things. Whereas the philosophers acknowledged an apparent rule of chance, they insisted that it could be escaped or overcome by rational thought. The Stoic endorsement of divination, for example, was not a concession to popular credulity but an acceptance of a rational technique for knowing the order of things by discerning its natural signs. According to the first-century C.E. Stoic Epictetus, true philosophy and piety are one and the same thing (*Ench.* 31, 1).

The strength of early Hellenistic philosophy was its pragmatic simplicity and democratic reasonableness, its ability to function as a practical guide for any reflective person, helping its followers to cope with a fortuitous world. But this strength was also its weakness, for in addressing the pressing ethical concerns of Hellenistic existence, Hellenistic philosophy abandoned cosmological speculation, resting its case upon the traditional cosmological assumptions of the pre-Socratic philosophers—Epicurus upon Democritus and Zeno upon Heraclitus. In its rejection of, rationalization of, or studied indifference to an external rule of Tyche, Hellenistic philosophies often lacked the insights of the lively mythological objectifications of Hellenistic existence. Consequently, they tended toward sophistry or, as was the case with the later Stoics, toward an uncritical eclecticism, indiscriminately reducing all manner of spiritual claims to the philosophical assumption of a First Principle. Increasingly, Hellenistic philosophy became either popularized and somewhat trivialized, or overly specialized and finally inaccessible to much of the populace.

Divination and the Cosmic Order of Things

Divination was the most pervasive example of Hellenistic piety. Like philosophy, it assumed a finite and rational cosmos in which everything, animate and inanimate, mortals and gods, was subject to the same sympathetic forces. Diviners revealed an order of things by claiming to "read" or understand the sympathetic parallels within the cosmos.

The Roman author Cicero (106–43 B.C.E.), in *De Divinatione,* one of the most important works on divination from the Hellenistic period, described this practice as an ancient and universal art:

> There is an ancient belief, handed down to us even from mythical times and firmly established by the general agreement of the Roman people and of all nations, that divination of some kind exists among men; this the Greeks call *mantikē*—that is, the foresight and knowledge of future events. A really splendid and helpful thing it is—if only such a faculty exists—since by its means men may approach very near to the power of the gods. And, just as we Romans have done many other things better than the Greeks, so have we excelled them in giving to this most extraordinary gift a name, which we have derived from *divi,* a word meaning "gods," whereas, according to Plato's interpretation, they have derived it from *furor,* a word meaning "frenzy." Now I am aware of no people, however refined and learned or however savage and ignorant, which does not think that signs are given of future events, and that certain persons can recognize those signs and foretell events before they occur.
>
> *Div.* I, 1, 1

Although Cicero finally rejected the practice of divination in favor of philosophical inquiry, he understood this ancient art as a desirable human faculty that most nearly achieved divine power. As Ptolemy also said of astrology:

> What could be more conducive to well-being, pleasure, and in general satisfaction than this kind of forecast [*prognōsis*], by which we gain full view of things human and divine?   *Tet.* I, 3, 10

Cicero's antagonist, Quintus, argued that divination generally was the "foreknowledge and foretelling of events that happen by chance" (*Div.* I, 5, 9; I, 55, 125)—that is, by *heimarmenē,* or fate (I, 55, 125). *Heimarmenē,* he continued, is "an orderly succession of causes wherein cause is linked to cause and each cause of itself produces an effect" (I, 55, 125). Since, Quintus concluded,

> all things happen by Fate, if there were a man whose soul could discern the links that join each cause with every other cause, then

surely he would never be mistaken in any prediction he might make. . . . [For] he who knows the causes of future events necessarily knows what every future event will be . . . , [for] the evolution of time is like the unwinding of a cable: it creates nothing new and only unfolds each event in its order.   *Div*. I, 56, 127

Divination was not so much the prediction of a temporal future as it was a conquest of ignorance concerning the cosmic or spatial order of things. This spatial law of inevitable causality negated any view of the future as temporal possibility.

Cicero identified two types of divination: "one which is allied with art; the other, which is devoid of art" or is "natural" (*Div*. I, 18, 34). Artificial divination, according to Cicero, proceeds by deduction based upon what can be known by observation, whereas natural or intuitive divination operates "under the influence of mental excitement (*Div*. I, 18, 34). The distinction between artificial and natural types of divination is somewhat arbitrary; the craft of the artificial diviner overlaps with the intuitive faculty of the natural diviner. Nevertheless, the differing techniques employed justify the typology.

Artificial Divination

Artificial divination attempted to discern deductively the sympathetic relationship of man and the cosmic order. In this type of divination, natural processes and their patterns were observed and construed as signatures of this order. For example, in theriomancy, or divination by animals, the Greeks observed the instinctual patterns of animals. In ornithomancy, or divination by birds, the diviner studied migratory patterns, characteristic calls, and flight patterns. Patterns of inanimate natural phenomena also afforded an unlimited range of possibilities for divination. In pyromancy, or divination by fire, diviners examined the patterns of nature exhibited in the brightness or configurations of flame and smoke. Similarly, the natural courses of springs and rivers were watched in hydromancy. To this day, vestiges of divination are preserved in rural folk wisdom concerning planting times and the exigencies of weather. In artificial divination, diviners, literate in the language of cosmic sympathy, presumed to "read" in the natural signs of the cosmos something of its order.

Astrology

Astrology was the most widespread and influential form of artificial divination in Hellenistic times. Its encompassing system of celestial universalism accorded well with post-Alexandrian transformations.[9] Based upon deduction from the obvious and observable effects of the sun and moon on terrestrial life, astrology was considered the most scientific and rational method of divination.[10]

Astrology is considered to have been systematized by the ancient Babylonians, who developed the twelve-house horoscope and the model of the seven planetary spheres, and who associated the observable regularity of the heavenly bodies with the natural processes of the cosmos.[11] Initially, the divination of the ancient Babylonians, or Chaldeans as they were known, had little to do with individuals. Instead, it was concerned with matters of social or political importance, such as weather, agriculture, war, prosperity, and the activities of the king as the representative of the country and its people.

The Hellenistic priests of Egypt applied Greek rules of mathematics and logical causality to astrology and elevated it to the position of a universal science. Because it emerged from the confluence of Babylonian, Egyptian, and Greek thought and was articulated finally in terms of Ptolemaic cosmology, astrology was the most Hellenistic form of divination. More than any other such form, it captured the Hellenistic imagination.[12]

Ptolemy's *Tetrabiblos,* written in the second century C.E., was a comprehensive summary of previous astronomical theory. It provided the definitive text for subsequent Western astrology.[13] Ptolemaic astrology, like its Babylonian forerunner, sought to apply the unchangeable, regular patterns of the heavenly bodies, predictable by astronomy, to seemingly fortuitous, unpredictable changes in the sublunar realm of the inhabited earth. Ptolemy's name for this sublunar transitoriness was "chance event" (*Tet.* 1, 2). As in Babylonia, the Hellenistic association of the superlunar and sublunar regions presumed the sympathetic relation of the macrocosm and the microcosm that provided for the "general harmony of organized nature."[14] By gaining access to "a full view of things human and divine" through astrology, an individual was able to outwit the effects of a capricious Tyche/Fortuna and secure at-homeness in the world.

On the one hand, astrology presupposed astronomy, the most advanced and exact of the Hellenistic sciences. Like philosophy, astrology epitomized the Greek faith in reason; in the face of the apparently fortuitous nature of human existence, there was a causal law of nature to which even deities were subject.[15] On the other hand, a basic presupposition of astrology was Greek myth, illustrated by the naming of celestial bodies after the gods and derivation of planetary characteristics from them.[16] It was probably this mythic aspect of astrology that accounted for its widespread popularity. Increasingly, however, its mathematical side propelled it from the realm of popular piety into a specialized art beyond the grasp of ordinary folk.

Alchemy

Alchemy, like astrology, extended cosmic patterns of sympathy to the material world by drawing an analogy between agricultural order and the transformation of material elements. The transformative growth of seed grain into cereal was mythologized as a natural growth from the womb of Mother Earth. The transformative growth of base metals into the nobler metals of silver and gold was mythologized as a growth deep within the ore-womb of Mother Earth, a process no less natural if more protracted. Through techniques of cultivation, the earth could be induced to produce a greater cereal yield and more quickly; similarly, alchemical practice sought to hasten an assumed natural transformatory growth of base metal into precious metal.[17]

In the West, alchemy emerged from the application of Greek philosophical principles to the metallurgical craft of Egypt.[18] The first clear reference to the art occurs in the first century c.e., when the Roman scholar Pliny wrote:

> There is . . . one method of making gold out of orpiment [yellow sulphide of arsenic]. . . . Hopes inspired by it had attracted the Emperor Gaius Caligula, who was extremely covetous for gold, and who consequently gave orders for a great weight of it to be smelted; and as a matter of fact it did produce excellent gold, but so small a weight of it that he found himself a loser.   *HN* XXXIII, 22, 79

The earliest surviving treatise on alchemical ideas is the *Physics and Mystics* from the late first or second century c.e., associated with the name of Democritus. From the second and third centuries, the *Corpus Hermeticum,* especially the tractates known as *The Krater* and the *Kore Kosmu,* employed alchemical imagery. And Zosimos of Panopolis, writing in the fourth century c.e., systematized earlier alchemical traditions just as Ptolemy had systematized those of astrology.

The alchemist shared the Hellenistic assumptions of sympathetic correspondence in the phenomenal world. All creation, inanimate and animate, plant and animal, is differentiated from a common *prima materia* that constantly undergoes natural transformation within the finite bounds of the cosmic "test tube." The alchemist, like the astrologer or the philosopher, sought to understand and appropriate these natural processes of the assumed order of things, whether his test tube was the laboratory vessel, the womb of the earth, or the cosmic circumference itself. According to alchemical theory, the effects of Fortune, arbitrary change, could be controlled and overcome. As Zosimos summarized:

> But Hermes and Zoroaster say that philosophers [i.e., the alchemists] as a class are superior to Fate because they neither rejoice in her good fortune, for they are master over pleasures, nor are they thrown by the evils she sends, as they always lead an inner life, nor do they accept the fair gifts she offers, since they look to end of ills.
> *On the Letter Omega,* 5[19]

Alchemy was almost always associated with astrology, and it contributed a dynamic element to an otherwise static cosmological system of correspondences between the celestial and the terrestrial realms. Saturn, described by Ptolemy as the coldest and darkest as well as the largest and heaviest of the celestial spheres, corresponded to the terrestrial *prima materia* of earth, ore, and lead. Through the reductive application of water and fire, or the influence of liquid (Mercury) and fire (Mars), a Saturnic nature was moved in the direction of silver (Moon) and gold (Sun). In the Ptolemaic cosmological table, Mercury and Mars are the neighbor planets of the Moon and the Sun, respectively, and consequently provide access to the lunar and solar realities in the movement from Saturn. This sympathetic correspondence between the alchemical and astrological systems was also understood to exist between plants (pharmacology), colors (chromatics), and numbers (numerology) as components of an integrated cosmic system.

Natural Divination

Natural divination, according to Cicero, is "devoid of art." Natural diviners forecast the future "unaided by reason or deduction or by

signs which have been observed and recorded . . . under the influence
of mental excitement, or of some free and unrestrained emotion" (*Div.*
I, 18, 34). The precedent for this type of divination was cleromancy,
divination by lot or chance. Cleromancy was an attempt to read directly the patterns of chance and to act accordingly. A specialized
example of cleromancy was cledonomancy, or divination by observing
an involuntary act of speech. Such an involuntary act was understood
to be a momentary possession by a god. A *cledon,* an omen contained
in a word or sound, was most reliable when uttered by those least
capable of calculating their effect, such as fools and children, calling to
mind the proverb, "out of the mouths of babes . . . ."

From cleromancy and its interpretation, the great Greek oracles
developed. Derived etymologically from *orare* (in Latin, to speak),
an oracle is a spoken omen or the interpretation of inspired speaking.
No oracle in the ancient world was better known or more influential
than the oracle of Apollo at Delphi.

The Delphic Oracle

According to the first-century B.C.E. Greek historian Diodorus Siculus, the oracle at Delphi was a chthonic oracle first discovered by
that earthy animal, the goat. "They say," he writes,

> that the manner of its discovery was the following. There is a chasm
> at this place where now is situated what is known as the "forbidden"
> sanctuary, and as goats had been wont to feed about this because
> Delphi had not as yet been settled, invariably any goat that ap-
> proached the chasm and peered into it would leap about in an
> extraordinary fashion and utter a sound quite different from what it
> was formerly wont to emit. The herdsman in charge of the goats
> marvelled at the strange phenomenon and having approached the
> chasm and peeped down it to discover what it was, had the same
> experience as the goats, for the goats began to act like beings pos-
> sessed and the goatherd also began to foretell future events. After
> this as the report was bruited among the people of the vicinity
> concerning the experience of those who approached the chasm, an
> increasing number of persons visited the place and, as they all tested
> it because of its miraculous character, whosoever approached the
> spot became inspired. For these reasons the oracle came to be re-
> garded as a marvel and to be considered the prophecy-giving shrine
> of Earth.   *Diod. Sic.* XVI, 26, 1–3

Diodorus's account illustrates the traditional Greek chthonic under-standing of sacrality as immanent. Rather than building their temples and sanctuaries at some convenient locale and then consecrating them to a particular deity, the Greeks constructed them at sacred places they discovered.[20]

The tradition reported by Diodorus understood the Delphic ora-cle to work through a medium who fell into a trance or became inspired, upon approaching the Delphic chasm. Subsequently the ora-cle was institutionalized to protect those possessed from the pull of the earth's depths. The Pythia, priestesses of the feminine Earth, were chosen to enter into trance on behalf of the supplicants. Diodorus continues:

> For some time all who wished to obtain a prophecy approached the chasm and made their prophetic replies to one another; but later, since many were leaping down into the chasm under the influence of their frenzy, and all disappeared, it seemed best to the dwellers in that region, in order to eliminate the risk, to station one woman there as a single prophetess for all and to have the oracle told through her. And for her a contrivance was devised which she could safely mount, then become inspired and give prophecies to those who so desired. And this contrivance had three supports and hence was called a tripod, and, I dare say, all the bronze tripods which are constructed even to this day are made in imitation of this contrivance. *Diod. Sic.* XVI, 26, 4–5

However, as archaeological and geological investigations have un-covered no trace of a chasm at Delphi, Diodorus was probably speak-ing metaphorically of inspiration by the very essence of the earth at this ancient chthonic oracle. The Priestess was protected by her tri-pod and ritual preparation from the depths of her ecstatic experience rather than from the literal depths of the chasm.

A second tradition concerning the origin of Delphi was preserved by the tragedian Euripides. According to Euripides also (*Iphigenia in Tauris,* 1234–1283), the oracle at Delphi was originally an oracle of Earth but involved oneiromancy, divination by dreams. This noctur-nal activity became intolerable to the Olympian solar deity, Apollo, who wished to rule Delphi himself and was finally granted his wish by his father, Zeus. The *Homeric Hymn to Pythian Apollo* recounts a similar tale in which Apollo established himself at Delphi by slaying Python, the dragon-guardian of the Earth oracle. The chthonic oracle of Delphi thus became the oracle of Olympian Apollo.[21] This account of Apollo's usurpation of the ancient Earth oracle reflected its formal Olympianization, and the priests of Apollo consequently came to share the site with the Pythia.

The oracle could be consulted only on the proper day, once a month. In order to consult the oracle, it was necessary to pay a fee by means of a preliminary offering. This offering entitled the questioner to approach the altar and offer a blood sacrifice of sheep or goats. Divination by sprinkling cold water over a goat established the presence of the god and his readiness to be questioned. After the priestess had first drunk from and been purified in the nearby Castalian Spring, she entered the temple. Mounting her tripod, she gave inspired responses to questions.

The traditions surrounding the development from the ancient Earth oracle at Delphi of an institutionalized oracle of Apollo exemplify a movement from immediate relations to chthonic forms of sacrality and spontaneous divination toward ritualized appearances of deity and institutionalized cults presided over by a specialized priesthood. The oracle belonged to the old world of traditional cosmology and its accessible deities. The Ptolemaic structures of the cosmos, in which the terrestrial presence of the gods could no longer be assumed, provided the conditions for later forms of cult epiphany.

Dreaming

Dreaming is one of the most ancient techniques of divination. Homer distinguished between dreams that "find no fulfillment" and those which "bring true issues to pass (*Od.* 19, 560–566). A theoretical grounding for this Homeric association of predictive dream with truth was first suggested by Plato. In the *Republic,* Socrates suggests that although dreams generally reflect a bestial element in human nature, moderate living and justness of the mind would permit the soul in sleep to grasp the truth (*Resp.* IX, 571–572).

This Platonic argument was repeated for the Hellenistic world by Quintus in Cicero's *De Divinatione.* Quintus clearly stated that moral purity of the soul was a necessary condition for oneiromancy as for all divinatory practice (*Div.* I, 53, 121). "It is the healthy soul and not the sickly body," Quintus concluded, "that has the power of divination" (*Div.* I, 23, 82).

The only complete work on dreams to survive from antiquity is the *Oneirocritica* of Artemidorus from the second century C.E. Like Plato, Artemidorus understood that a morally pure soul could discern dreams through its true place in the cosmic order of things. The existence and recognition of significant dreams empirically confirmed the true self's systemic relationship with and consequent access to this larger order.

Artemidorus wrote his book as an apology for *mantikē,* or divination generally, with dreams as a case in point (I, *pro.*). His systematic discussion established him as the authority for subsequent oneirological practice,[22] just as Ptolemey's systematic reflections upon extant astronomical theory established him as the authority for subsequent astrological practice.

Artemidorus's dream theory presupposed the threefold classification of dreams common in antiquity: the *chrematismos* or oracular dream, the *enhypnion* or nonpredictive dream, and the *oneiros* or predictive dream.[23] Artemidorus was a "professional" dream specialist concerned with "ordinary" dreaming as either predictive or nonpredictive. He omitted the *chrematismos* from his considerations, as it belonged to the specialized practices of the so-called incubation cults and rarely occurred apart from their domain.[24] Consequently, he was not concerned with the relation of dream to religious practice as was his contemporary Aelius Aristides, for whom dreams were media of divine revelation.

The *Sacred Tales* of the rhetorician and sophist Aelius Aristides (circa 117 or 129–181 or later) is an account of his protracted illness, including a record of oracular dreams in which the god Asclepius prescribed cures while Aristides was a patient at the Asclepium of Pergamum.[25] This account, more than the dream book of Artemidorus, has captured the imagination of modern interpreters.[26] Aristides states his theory of oracular dreams at the beginning of his *Sacred Tales:*

> Each of our days, as well as our nights, has a story if someone, who was present at them, wished either to record the events or to narrate the providence of the god, wherein he revealed somethings openly in his own presence and others by the sending of dreams.
>
> *Sacred Tales* I, 3[27]

Such oracular dreaming was employed for the management of crises resulting from misfortune, the most oppressive of which was illness.[28]

Aristides had decided "to submit truly to the God [Asclepius], truly as to a doctor, and to do in silence whatever he wishes" (*Sacred Tales* I, 4, 57). He did so throughout a long series of illnesses, even when Asclepius gave advice contrary to that of Aristides' attending physicians (*Sacred Tales* I, 63), or contrary to common sense (*Sacred Tales* II, 7). Although he never recovered from his maladies, he continued to confess "the healing god, Asclepius" as his savior (*Sacred Tales,* passim).

Asclepius and Healing

Asclepius was known to Homer as a mortal physician; his emergence as a savior deity was primarily a Hellenistic phenomenon. Whether he is understood as an apotheosized mortal or as chthonic deity, Asclepius's rise to universal acclaim began in the age of Alexander, who reportedly paid homage to him. According to the mid-second-century C.E. Greek traveler, Pausanias,

> the natives [of Gortys in Arcadia] also say that Alexander the son of Philip dedicated to Asclepius his breastplate and spear. The breastplate and the head of the spear are still there to-day.
>
> *Paus.* VIII, 28, 1

At the beginning of the third century B.C.E. under the sanction of the Delphic oracle, Asclepius was one of the first "foreign" gods to be received in Rome. By the fourth century C.E., over 400 sanctuaries had been dedicated to Asclepius throughout the Hellenistic world. Outposts of his influence survived into the fifth century, when most finally succumbed to Christianization.

Although the historical origin of Asclepius was almost certainly in Thessaly, by Hellenistic times his birth in Epidaurus was generally accepted.[29] According to the generally agreed-upon elements of Hellenistic myth, Asclepius was born of Apollo and a mortal mother, Coronis. As an infant he was rescued from danger (the nature of which varies according to the version) by his father and was raised by the centaur Chiron, who taught him healing. Asclepius died a mortal, but through the intervention of the gods was resurrected to the status of a demi-god. He was known to suppliants by his epiphanies in their healing dreams.

An official Epidaurean record of cures bears the following superscription:

> God and Good Fortune (*Tycha agatha*)
> Cures of Apollo and Asclepius[30]

This superscription clearly associates a divine Asclepius with his father, Apollo, also a god of healing. Similarly, according to Aristides, statues of Good Fortune and of the Good God (Asclepius) stood side by side in the temple of Asclepius at Pergamum (*Sacred Tales* I, 10–11); for Aristides, Asclepius was "the arbiter of fate" (*Sacred Tales* II, 31). This association of "Good Fortune," with the divine cures of Asclepius and Apollo suggests a view of illness as the effect of capricious fortune, and consequently as a cosmic metaphor for the malaise of Hellenistic existence. In contrast to the "scientific" medicine of the fifth-century B.C.E. physician Hippocrates, the medicine of Asclepius was divine and sought to heal this existential malaise and its physical symptoms.

In the rite of incubation, the sick were first admitted to the Asclepian sanctuary for initial purification and preliminary sacrifices. The *therapeutae,* or Asclepian priests, would determine the presence of the god by divination and announce his invitation to the suppliant. So bidden, the sick would spend the night in the *abaton* or inner sanctuary, where the god would appear to them in a dream or vision, often in his theriomorphic aspect as a serpent or a dog, to touch the afflicted part of the body or to give a therapeutic instruction. The *therapeutae* then would interpret and record the dream, which was the mystery of the cure. These incubation practices survived into Christianity, where a local saint was substituted for the healing god Asclepius.[31]

The following typical accounts of Asclepian cures, dating from the latter part of the fourth century B.C.E., are taken from a stele recording official testimonials at Epidaurus, where they were prominently displayed to attract the notice of visitors to the shrine:

A man whose fingers, with the exception of one, were paralyzed, came as a suppliant to the god. While looking at the tablets in the temple he expressed incredulity regarding the cures and scoffed at the inscriptions. But in his sleep he saw a vision. It seemed to him that, as he was playing at dice below the Temple and was about to cast the dice, the god appeared, sprang upon his hand, and stretched out his [the patient's] fingers. When the god had stepped aside it seemed to him [the patient] that he [the patient] bent his hand and stretched out all his fingers one by one. When he had straightened them all, the god asked him if he would still be incredulous of the inscriptions on the tablets in the Temple. He answered that he would not. "Since, then, formerly you were incredulous of the cures, though they were not

incredible, for the future," he said, "your name shall be 'Incredulous.' " When day dawned he walked out sound.

• • •

Ambrosia of Athens, blind of one eye. She came as a suppliant to
the god. As she walked about in the Temple she laughed at some of
the cures as incredible and impossible, that the lame and the blind
should be healed by merely seeing a dream. In her sleep she had a
vision. It seemed to her that the god stood by her and said that he
would cure her, but that in payment he would ask her to dedicate to
the Temple a silver pig as a memorial of her ignorance. After saying
this, he cut the diseased eyeball and poured in some drug. When
day came she walked out sound.

IG, IV, 1, nos. 121–22, 3–4[32]

From these accounts it is clear that soteriological transformation
in the Hellenistic world sympathetically embraced the inner realm of
dream and vision as well as the physical realm of bodily dysfunction.
Within the parameters of the finite cosmos, sympathetic correspondence between inner and outer, human and divine, animate and inanimate, psychic and somatic were considered natural. Soteriological
transformation through the ritual epiphany of a personal savior not
only identifies the later Asclepian rites as a genuinely Hellenistic
form but also associates this medicine with that exemplar of Hellenistic religiosity, the Mysteries.

Specialization and Senility

Hellenistic piety, then, preserved patterns of the sacred out of which
the characteristically Hellenistic strategies of existence emerged. Traditional folk piety also persisted as a religious expression in its own
right, responding to and adapting to the order of a new world.
Viewed from the perspective of the Hellenistic transformations, however, survivals of traditional folk piety displayed two tendencies: specialization and senility.

The expressions of piety that grappled successfully with the for-
tunes of existence in the Hellenistic world did so by keeping pace with
an explosion of scientific, technological, and conceptual knowledge.
Technical specialization was necessary for the mathematical and technological competency demanded by the systemization of such practices
as astrology, alchemy, and the professional interpretation of dreams.

A second type of specialization was exemplified by technicians of the sacred, such as the professionals of Delphi and Epidaurus, at whose hands sacred order emerged as an esoteric knowledge.[33]

However, some of the traditional modes of piety were increasingly regarded as senile, especially by the philosophers.[34] Plutarch discussed the deterioration of folk piety in his *The Obsolescence of Oracles*. First, he reasoned, there was less need for oracles because the population had decreased—a questionable explanation at best. Second, Plutarch attributed the decline of oracles to the fact that they were controlled by demons or demi-gods rather than directly by gods. Because these demi-gods were subject to mortality, they, like the oracles over which they presided, had simply grown old.

As Apuleius makes clear toward the end of his novel, traditional piety is no longer of avail in avoiding "cruel and envious Fortune" (*Met.* X, 23–24). However, piety in service to the Mysteries is of profit (*Met.* XI, 30).

Notes

1. Javier Teixidor, *The Pagan God: Popular Religion in the Greco-Roman Near East* (Princeton, N.J.: Princeton University Press, 1977), pp. 6, 11.

2. Martin P. Nilsson, *Greek Folk Religion* (New York: Harper, 1961), p. 73.

3. See S. R. F. Price, *Rituals and Power: The Roman Imperial Cult in Asia Minor* (Cambridge: Cambridge University Press, 1984), pp. 15–16.

4. Nilsson, pp. 22–41.

5. On the "Philosophical Religion" of classical Greece, see Walter Burkert, *Greek Religion,* trans. John Raffan (Cambridge, Mass.: Harvard University Press, 1985), pp. 305–337.

6. See the discussion on Epicurean philosophy and fate by William Chase Greene, *Moira: Fate, Good, and Evil in Greek Thought* (Gloucester, Mass.: Peter Smith, 1968), pp. 333–337.

7. F. C. Grant (trans.), *Hellenistic Religions,* in The Library of Liberal Arts (Indianapolis, Ind.: Bobbs-Merrill, 1953), pp. 152–153.

8. See the discussion on Stoic philosophy and fate by Greene, pp. 337–354.

9. Franz Cumont, *Astrology and Religion Among the Greeks and Romans,* trans. J. B. Baker (New York: Dover, 1960), p. 32.

10. Frederick H. Cramer, *Astrology in Roman Law and Politics,* Mem-

oirs of the American Philosophical Society, vol. 37 (Philadelphia: American Philosophical Society, 1954), p. 4.

11. Cumont, p. 12; Cramer, pp. 4–5.

12. Cramer, pp. 7–8.

13. Cumont, p. 81

14. Cumont, p. xvi.

15. Cramer, p. 281.

16. Cramer, p. 4.

17. See Mircea Eliade, *The Forge and the Crucible,* trans. Stephen Corrin (New York: Harper & Row, 1971), chap. 4.

18. Arthur J. Hopkins, *Alchemy, Child of Greek Philosophy* (New York: Columbia University Press, 1934), pp. 7–8.

19. *Zosimos of Panopolis on the Letter Omega,* Howard M. Jackson (trans. and ed.) (Missoula, Mont.: Scholars Press, 1978).

20. Vincent Scully emphasizes this point in his excellent study of Greek sacred architecture, *The Earth, the Temple and the Gods,* rev. ed. (New York: Praeger, 1969), chap. 1.

21. See Joseph Fontenrose, *Python, A Study of Delphic Myth and Its Origins,* (Berkeley, Calif.: University of California Press, 1959).

22. Angelo Brelich, "The Place of Dreams in the Religious World Concept of the Greeks," in G. E. von Grunebaum and Roger Caillois (eds.), *The Dream and Human Societies* (Berkeley, Calif.: University of California Press, 1966), p. 294.

23. Charles A. Behr, *Aelius Aristides and The Sacred Dream* (Amsterdam: A. M. Hakkert, 1968), p. 174.

24. Claes Blum, *Studies in the Dream-Book of Artemidorus* (Uppsala, Sweden: Almquist & Wiksells, 1936), pp. 68–69; Behr, p. 174.

25. Charles A. Behr (trans.), *P. Aelius Aristides, The Complete Works,* vol. II: *Orations XVII–LIII* (Leiden: E. J. Brill, 1981), Orations XLVII–LII.

26. See, for example, A.-J. Festugière, *Personal Religion Among the Greeks* (Berkeley, Calif.: University of California Press, 1954), chap. VI; E. R. Dodds, *The Greeks and The Irrational* (Berkeley, Calif.: University of California Press, 1951), pp. 113–116; Howard Clark Kee, *Miracle in the Early Christian World* (New Haven, Conn.: Yale University Press, 1983), pp. 93–103.

27. Trans. Charles A. Behr.

28. Burkert, pp. 264–268.

29. Emma J. and Ludwig Edelstein, *Asclepius: A Collection and Interpretation of the Testimonies.* vol. II (New York: Arno Press, 1975), pp. 71–72.

30. Edelstein, vol. I, Testamony 423, p. 229.

31. See the classic study in English by Mary Hamilton, *Incubation or the Cure of Disease in Pagan Temples and Christian Churches* (St. Andrews, Scotland: W. C. Henderson and Sons, 1906).

32. Edelstein, vol. I, Testamony 423, 3, and 4, p. 230. Compare also the accounts from medieval and modern Christianity in Hamilton, parts II and III.

33. G. E. R. Lloyd, *Magic, Reason and Experience: Studies in the Origins and Development of Greek Science* (Cambridge: Cambridge University Press, 1979), p. 227.

34. See Harold W. Attridge, "The Philosophical Critique of Religion under the Early Empire," *Aufstieg und Niedergang der Römischen Welt* II, 16, 1 (Berlin and New York: Walter de Gruyter, 1978), pp. 45–78.

Selected Bibliography

Traditional Greek Piety

A.-J. Festugière, *Greek Piety,* trans. Herbert Jennings Rose (New York: Norton, 1969).

————, *A History of Greek Religion,* 2nd ed., trans. F. J. Fielden (New York: Norton, 1964).

————, *Personal Religion Among the Greeks* (Berkeley, Calif.: University of California Press, 1954).

Martin P. Nilsson, *Greek Folk Religion* (New York: Harper, 1961).

Javier Teixidor, *The Pagan God: Popular Religion in the Greco-Roman Near East* (Princeton, N.J.: Princeton University Press, 1977).

Robert L. Wilken, *The Christians as the Romans Saw Them* (New Haven, Conn.: Yale University Press, 1984), chap. III.

Hellenistic Philosophy

E. Vernon Arnold, *Roman Stoicism* (New York: Humanities Press, 1958).

C. Bailey, *The Greek Atomists and Epicurus* (Oxford: Clarendon Press, 1928), is the classic work on the Epicureans.

John Dillon, *The Middle Platonists: 80* B.C. *to* A.D. *220,* (Ithaca, N.Y.: Cornell University Press, 1977).

A.-J. Festugière, *Epicurus and His Gods* (Oxford: Basil Blackwell, 1955).

George D. Hadzits, *Lucretius and His Influences* (New York: Longmans, 1935).

A. A. Long, *Hellenistic Philosophy* (New York: Charles Scribner's Sons, 1974).

Max Pohlenz, *Die Stoa, Geschichte einer geistigen Bewegung,* 2 vols. (Göttingen, Germany: Vandenhoeck and Ruprecht, 1964), is the classic work on the Stoics.

John M. Rist, *Stoic Philosophy* (London: Cambridge University Press, 1969).

Jason L. Saunders (ed.), *Greek and Roman Philosophy After Aristotle* (New York: Free Press, 1966).

Divination

Cicero, *De Divinatione*, trans. W. A. Falconer, in the Loeb Classical Library, vol. xx (Cambridge, Mass.: Harvard University Press, 1923).

W. R. Halliday, *Greek Divination: A Study of Its Methods and Principles* (Chicago: Argonaut, 1967).

Astrology

Frederick H. Cramer, *Astrology in Roman Law and Politics,* Memoirs of the American Philosophical Society, vol. 37 (Philadelphia: American Philosophical Society, 1954) is an excellent introduction to Hellenistic astrology.

Franz Cumont, *Astrology and Religion Among the Greeks and Romans,* trans. J. B. Baker (New York: Dover, 1960) is the classical study.

Ptolemy, *Tetrabiblos,* trans. F. E. Robbins, in the Loeb Classical Library (Cambridge, Mass.: Harvard University Press, 1940).

Alchemy

Mircea Eliade, *The Forge and the Crucible,* trans. Stephen Corrin (New York: Harper & Row, 1971), includes an excellent general bibliography on alchemy, updated by the author in "The Forge and the Crucible: A Postscript," *History of Religions* 8 (1968), pp. 74–88.

E. J. Holmyard, *Alchemy* (Baltimore: Penguin Books, 1968), offers an excellent historical overview of alchemy.

A. J. Hopkins, *Alchemy, Child of Greek Philosophy* (New York: Columbia University Press, 1934).

Howard M. Jackson (trans. and ed.), *Zosimos of Panopolis on the Letter Omega* (Missoula, Mont.: Scholars Press, 1978).

C. G. Jung, *Psychology and Alchemy,* trans. R. F. C. Hull, in *Collected Works 12,* The Bollingen Series, 2nd ed., (Princeton, N.J.: Princeton University Press, 1968), is a psychological interpretation.

Jack Lindsay, *The Origins of Alchemy in Greco-Roman Egypt* (London: Frederick Muller, 1970), is a thorough study of the subject that includes a comprehensive bibliography.

Joseph Needham, *Science and Civilization in China* vol. 5, part II (Cambridge: Cambridge University Press, 1974), pp. 15–29.

Dreams in Late Antiquity

Charles A. Behr, *Aelius Aristides and The Sacred Tales* (Amsterdam: A. M. Hakkert, 1968).

————(trans.), *P. Aelius Aristides: The Complete Works,* vol. II: *Orations XVII–LII* (Leiden: E. J. Brill, 1981).

Claes Blum, *Studies in the Dream-Book of Artemidorus* (Uppsala, Sweden: Almquist & Wiksells, 1936).

Robert J. White, *The Interpretation of Dreams: Oneirocritica by Artemidorus,* Noyes Classical Studies (Park Ridge, N.J.: Noyes Press, 1975).

The Delphic Oracle

Robert Flacelière, *Greek Oracles,* trans. Douglas Garman (London: Elak Books, 1965).

Joseph Fontenrose, *Python: A Study of Delphic Myth and Its Origins* (Berkeley, Calif.: University of California Press, 1959).

————, *The Delphic Oracle, Its Responses and Operations with a Catalogue of Responses* (Berkeley, Calif.: University of California Press, 1978).

H. W. Parke, *Greek Oracles* (London: Hutchinson Library, 1967).

H. W. Parke and D. E. W. Wornell, *The Delphic Oracle,* 2 vols. (Oxford: Basil Blackwell, 1956).

Asclepius

Emma J. and Ludwig Edelstein, *Asclepius: A Collection and Interpretation of the Testimonies* (New York: Arno Press, 1975), is indispensable for any study of Asclepius.

Mary Hamilton, *Incubation or The Cure of Disease in Pagan Temple and Christian Churches* (St. Andrews, Scotland: W. C. Henderson and Sons, 1906).

C. Kerényi, *Asklepios: Archetypal Image of the Physician's Existence,* trans. Ralph Manheim, The Bollingen Series, (Princeton, N.J.: Princeton: Princeton University Press, 1959).

C. A. Meier, *Ancient Incubation and Modern Psychotherapy,* trans. Monica Curtis (Evanston, Ill.: Northwestern University Press, 1967).

3

The Mysteries and the Sovereignty of the Feminine

Traditional techniques of folk piety had been adapted in response to the aimlessness of existence that characterized the Hellenistic world. None of these traditional practices served, however, to transform the perception of this existence. In fact, Lucius's involvement with magic, one such practice, marked the beginning of his problems, and his "heroic" efforts to find a transformatory antidote did not lead him any closer to his goal. Increasingly, an accessible order of things could no longer be assumed; a transformation was required. Only when Lucius abandoned his self-assertive attempts to discover the means of transformation and placed himself solely in the providential hands of Isis was he led beyond traditional piety and transformed into his full humanity through the Mysteries of the Great Goddess.

Mystery Deities

Although the structures of piety continued as a popular stratum of Hellenistic religious thought, this period was marked by a revival of interest in the ancient chthonic "Mystery" cults. Broadly speaking, these Mysteries involved an initiation in which the problematic nature of an existence ruled by Tyche/Fortuna was not denied, escaped, or controlled, but rather transformed into an existence ruled by a goddess in her guise of "True Fortune."

The deities of the Hellenistic Mysteries were not new—they had been known from the earliest times—but were themselves transformed by and into their Hellenistic roles. Although the historical origin of each was still remembered as Greek, Egyptian, or Syrian, locale became less important; for with Hellenistic internationalism, each had become a universal deity. Thus, all the world was invited to Eleusis to become initiated into the Mysteries of Demeter, and the Egyptian Isis revealed to Lucius that her name and divinity were "adored throughout all the world."

As a result, a sacred order of things was no longer assumed to be immanent in a particular terrestrial realm or locale, but was elevated to the universal locus of the celestial realm. The presence of a divine natural order as assumed by traditional piety was supplanted by cult epiphanies of deities able to bridge the Ptolemaic image of the cosmic abyss and overcome the separation of humans from the gods. This new epiphany of the deity deposed the regional cosmic rule of Zeus, Poseidon, and Hades at once. As Isis revealed to Lucius, she was not only "mother of all things, mistress and governess of all the elements," but also "chief of the powers divine." She ruled not only the chthonic realm, as "queen of all that are in hell," but now also the celestial sphere, as "principal of them that dwell in heaven" (*Met.* XI, 5.). The goddess became sole sovereign of the cosmos and all therein, and only through her sacred rites could humans come to their at-homeness in terms of the complex Ptolemaic image of world.

In the myths of the Mysteries, these transformed deities are represented as wanderers whose journeys lead them from an existence of humanlike suffering to a transformed existence as celestial saviors. For Hellenistic existence the story of the wanderings, sufferings, and final homecoming of the universal goddess offered the possibility that one's own wandering and suffering might come to an end in a soteriological homecoming under her providential protection. Her story became the paradigm of salvation for the individual initiate and offered a transformed life to those willing to follow the spiritual path of her Mystery. Through initiation into her cult, the public myth of the deity was transformed into mystery gnosis, a ritualized knowledge of transformed human existence as at-homeness in the world.

The Mysteries

Initiates into the Mysteries were forbidden to speak of their initiation. As expressed in the seventh-century B.C.E. *Homeric Hymn to Demeter,* the revelations of the goddess to the Eleusinians are "awful mysteries which no one may in any way transgress or pry into or utter, for deep awe of the gods checks the voice" (lines 478–479). Similarly, as Lucius demurs, following his initiation into the Mysteries of Isis:

> Thou wouldest peradventure demand, thou studious reader, what was said and done there: verily I would tell thee if it were lawful for me to tell, thou wouldst know if it were convenient for thee to hear; but both thy ears and my tongue should incur the like pain of rash curiosity.   *Met.* XI, 23

The famous case of Alcibiades, a respected fifth-century B.C.E. Athenian general, provides one of the few records of any serious breach of silence concerning the Mysteries (*Thuc.* 6, 27–29). The charge against Alcibiades was reported in the Hellenistic period by Plutarch:

> Thessalus, son of Cimon, of the deme Laciadae, impeaches Alcibiades, son of Cleinias, of the deme Scambonidae, for committing crime against the goddesses of Eleusis, Demeter and Core, by mimicking the mysteries and showing them forth to his companions in his own house, wearing a robe such as the High Priest wears when he shows forth the sacred secrets to the initiates, and calling himself High Priest, Pulytion Torch-bearer, and Theodorus, of the deme Phegaea, Herald, and hailing the rest of his companions as Mystae and Epoptae, contrary to the laws and institutions of the Eumolpidae, Heralds, and Priests of Eleusis.   *Vit. Alc.* XXII, 3

Alcibiades was convicted of this charge, and according to Plutarch's report, his property was confiscated in his absence; moreover, "it was also decreed that his name should be publically cursed by all priests and priestesses" (*Vit. Alc.* XXII, 4).

Alcibiades was not accused of revealing secrets to noninitiates, however, but rather was charged with "mocking" the Eleusinian Mysteries by performing them in private houses (*Thuc.* 6, 27–28). With Thucydides, Plutarch saw Alcibiades's action as a parody of the Eleusinian Mysteries, that is, as a profanization of the Eleusinian goddess (*Thuc.* 6, 60–61; *Vit. Alc.* XIX, 1).

It may be inferred from the case of Alcibiades that the conundrum of the Mysteries had less to do with kept secrets or occult knowledge—although this may have been a formal aspect—than with desecrating the ineffable mystery of an unveiled deity. The awe-inspiring epiphany, a manifestation of inexpressible sacrality itself, could not be disclosed without profanization. This would explain the deep reverence and respect shown the Mysteries by the initiate, the uninitiate, and the apostate alike. As the Roman poet Ovid wrote:

> Who would dare to publish to the profane the rites of Ceres, or the great ceremonies devised in Samothrace? Keeping silence is but a small virtue, but to speak what should not be uttered is a heinous crime. *Ars Am.* 2, 601–604

It has been customary to understand the contents of mystery initiation in terms of three categories: the *legomena,* or "that which was said"; the *drōmena,* or "that which was done"; and the *deiknymena,* or "that which was shown."[1] There has been much speculation concerning what secrets might have been shown and told to initiates and what acts might have been done in their presence. These three categories, however, like the modern categories of myth, ritual, and symbol, are merely academic conventions that provide a convenient if nontechnical framework for discussion of the Mysteries. This understanding of the Mysteries is nowhere attested to in antiquity, however, and such generalizations are best avoided in favor of what is actually known of the Mystery cults.

Lucian, the second-century C.E. satirist, wrote that no mystery was ever celebrated without dancing (*Salt.* 15). Public celebrations of the Mysteries consisted primarily of elaborate processions, the stylized dance of ritual. These "dances" ranged from the ecstatic romp of the Dionysian *maenads* through the hillsides of Greece, as dramatized by Euripides in *The Bacchae,* to the majestic state-sanctioned procession from Athens to Eleusis of the devotees of Demeter. These processions publically expressed the soteriological promises of a well-known Mystery myth to curious onlookers, while at the same time preparing the initiates for induction into the Mysteries. The Mysteries expressed, therefore, both an everyday and a sacred content in which a public level of understanding might be superceded by initiatory insight.

In contrast to traditional piety, which belonged to social convention, initiation into the Mysteries was both voluntary and individual.

The preparation was often described as twofold: *katharsis* and *systasis*.[2] *Katharsis* was the preliminary ritual cleansing or purification of the initiate. This cleansing made the initiate worthy of the *systasis*, the collection or assembling of the initiates or *mystae* for the ritual dance or procession. Embracing preparatory rites and sacrifices, the *systasis* would also serve as the initiates' formal introduction into the company of the Mysteries.

The procession itself, whether frenzied or sedate, dramatically enacted both the wanderings of mortals under the buffetings of Tyche, and the paradigmatic wanderings of the cult deity. In its ritualized presentation, the initiates' wandering was no longer aimless but ecstatic (in Greek, *ekstasis*, meaning "a standing outside of oneself"). The initiate was now prepared to stand outside the old Tyche-dominated self, the old world, to be reborn through mystery initiation into the providential world ordered by the cult deity.

The sequence of the initiation repeated a ritual movement from the profane to the sacred: the purification of the *mystae* (*katharsis*), the formation of the procession from their gathering (*systasis*), the procession of the gathered *mystae* from the midst of the public arena to the sacred precincts (*temenos*) of the cult deity, and finally, the encounter with the manifest sacred—initiation (*teletē*) in the presence of divine epiphany. No longer was the initiate homeless in the midst of a chaotic, labyrinthian world: through initiation, the rule of that world was revealed as that of divine providence. The cosmic abyss that separated humans from the gods had been bridged, and their at-homeness in the world and with the gods had been established.

The Eleusinian Mysteries

The primary example of a Greek-based mystery in the Hellenistic era is the revival and expanded popularity of the famous Eleusinian Mysteries of Demeter.[3] Eleusis is located on the sea at the edge of the fertile Thriasian Plain, fourteen miles west of Athens. By the seventh century B.C.E., the city had been annexed by Athens, yet the Eleusians retained control of their Mysteries. These two cities remained the dominant sister cities of Attica: Athens was the political, social, and intellectual center, Eleusis the center of the Mysteries; the one, champion of the traditional Olympian spirit, the other, champion of the ancient chthonic spirit.

Exactly when Eleusis was incorporated by Athens into greater

Attica is disputed. However, this ancient fortified city and the fecund plain it controlled was the last territory to be annexed, and clearly the most important. *The Sacred Way,* the sole land route between Athens and Eleusis, not only united the two cities commercially and politically but emphasized their separation, as its name referred to the Eleusinian privilege of position over the Mysteries. The influence of Eleusis through the annual celebration of the Mysteries of Demeter endured long after the demise of Athenian political dominance, to be finally eclipsed by Christianity in the fifth century c.e.

The Myth of Demeter

Demeter, associated with the great chthonic fertility goddesses indigenous to the Mediterranean region, was "officially" considered a member of the Olympian family by Homer, who reported her to be the daughter of Cronos and Rhea. Although devotion to Demeter was widespread, the Mysteries of the goddess remained bound to the sacred precincts of Eleusis, preserving the Greek notion of an immanent rather than conferred sacrality.

The familiar story of the rape of Demeter's daughter, Persephone, by Hades, god of the underworld, and the subsequent joyous reunion of mother and daughter is told in the *Homeric Hymn to Demeter.* Although dated from the seventh century b.c.e., this hymn remained the "official" story of the Eleusinian cult throughout its long history.[4]

The Homeric tale of Demeter and Persephone is clearly narrated in terms of the traditional cosmology. Its divine realms harmoniously centered around the cosmic flower,

> a thing of awe whether for deathless gods or mortal men to see:
> from its roots grew a hundred blooms and it smelled most sweetly,
> so that all wide heaven above and the whole earth and the sea's salt
> swell laughed for joy.   *Hymn Hom. Cer.* 10–14

As Persephone gathered flowers in the meadow, she reached out innocently toward this "marvellous, radiant flower," but "the wide-pathed earth yawned there in the plain" and Hades, Lord of the Underworld, "sprang out upon her" and carried her away. In bitterness and grief, Demeter wandered about searching for her daughter:

> Bitter pain seized her heart, and she rent the coverings upon her
> divine hair with her dear hands: her dark cloak she cast down from
> both her shoulders and sped, like a wildbird, over the firm land and
> yielding sea, seeking her child. . . . For nine days queenly Deo
> wandered over the earth with flaming torches in her hands, so
> grieved that she never tasted ambrosia and the sweet draught of
> nectar, nor sprinkled her body with water.
>
> *Hymn Hom. Cer.* 39–50

Stricken with grief at the loss of her daughter, Demeter fled the
gathering of the gods and wandered sorrowfully among the mortals.

On the tenth day of her search for Persephone, Demeter was met
by Hecate, a lunar goddess, who together with Helios, the sun, had
witnessed Hades's abduction of Persephone. Hecate told Demeter
"truly and shortly all I know" (line 58). Learning of the divine conspir-
acy in the abduction of her daughter, Demeter avoided the gathering
of the gods and, disguised as a disfigured old woman, arrived at
Eleusis: "And so I wandered and am come here" (line 133).

In her terrestrial incarnation the wandering goddess was discovered resting at the Kallichoron Well by the daughters of Celeus, Lord
of Eleusis. Their mother, Queen Metaneira, invited the disguised
goddess into their home as nurse for her newborn son, Demophoon.
In gratitude, Demeter raised the child as a god, by day anointing him
with ambrosia and by night hiding him in the fire to burn away his
mortality. Curious about her son's prodigious growth, Metaneira
spied upon Demeter and was horrified to see her son placed in the
midst of the hearth fire. She confronted "Queen Demeter," who
angrily revealed her true identity to the Queen of Eleusis.

The two mothers, each acting out of concern for her child, dramatized the conflict between the terrestrial and the celestial queens.
After this confrontation, Demeter left her terrestrial home and re-
sumed her wandering, for Demophoon was the child of Metaneira,
and Persephone was still absent.

At the bidding of the goddess, the people of Eleusis built "a
goodly temple for rich-haired Demeter and an altar upon the rising
hillock" to which the goddess retreated. Yet this new hospitality extended by the Eleusinians could not suffice as home for the Celestial
Queen, for she was still separated from her family: "Demeter sat
there apart from all the blessed gods and stayed, wasting with yearn-
ing for her deep-bosomed daughter" (line 305). Causing "a most
dreadful and cruel year for mankind over the all-nourishing earth"

(lines 305–306), Demeter deprived the Olympian deities of their sacrificial offerings. Because of the blight Demeter had imposed on agriculture, Zeus, who had originally consented to the marriage between his brother, Hades, and his daughter, Persephone, finally intervened to return the daughter to her mother for two-thirds of the year. The remaining one-third of the year, Persephone was the happy bride of Hades. Grateful for even this partial reunion with her daughter, Demeter restored the fertility of the earth so that once again, sacrifice could be offered the gods; and, as a special favor, she showed the Eleusinians "the conduct of her rites and taught them all her mysteries" (lines 473–476). Demeter was then called upon to "join the family of the gods" (line 460).

With Persephone's homecoming, Demeter was reunited with her divine family. In this Olympian metaphor of divine at-homeness, the parents, Zeus and Demeter, are harmoniously reconciled with their daughter, Persephone, and with their new son-in-law, Hades. Likewise, through this marriage, sky (Father Zeus), earth (Mother Demeter), and underworld (Uncle Hades) are also reunited. Even in its original context of traditional cosmology, the message is clear: with the harmonious at-homeness of the divine family, cosmic rift is overcome: blessed is the man who establishes his own home with the gods.

The Rites of Demeter

The famous public ritual of Demeter conducted annually in Athens and Eleusis could be witnessed even by casual spectators. As the *Homeric Hymn to Demeter* seems to distinguish between the well-known myth and the "awful mysteries" that Demeter taught to the Eleusinians, so the public rites were only preparatory to mystery initiation.

The public performance of the Eleusinian Mysteries began with the so-called Lesser Mysteries. Celebrated each spring in Athens, these Lesser Mysteries were dedicated to Persephone upon the occasion of her return to the underworld and had a vestigal relation to the *thalysia,* the ancient agrarian harvest festival of the gathering of grain prior to the draught of summer and its storage in subterranean silos.[5] These Lesser Mysteries involved ritual purification and public sacrifice, generally of a pig, sacred to the Mediterranean fertility goddesses. These rites were undoubtedly catechetical and established the worthiness of the participants for initiation into the Greater Mysteries of Demeter celebrated at Eleusis in the fall.

The celebration of the Lesser Mysteries in Athens was mythically justified as satisfying the desire of Heracles to be initiated.[6] This deference to an Athenian hero reflected the deference of Eleusis to Athenian political domination. Although the Eleusinians continued to preside over their Mysteries, eligibility for initiation was extended to the Athenians and later to all citizens of Attica. Thereafter, the Eleusinian rites had their official opening in this annual rite in Athens. Finally, eligibility for initiation became extended to all Greek-speaking suppliants.

The celebration of the Greater Mysteries, dedicated to Demeter, was in the latter part of September, the time of the *thesmophoria* or festival of fall planting.[7] It was consummated in the Telesterion, the Place of Perfection, within the sacred precincts of the Demeter sanctuary in Eleusis. To enable international participation in these Mysteries, a seldom-broken, fifty-five-day truce was called between all warring states. The festival lasted ten days, recalling the duration of Demeter's wandering in search of her abducted daughter before learning the truth from Hecate on the tenth day.

The first part of the festival of the Greater Mysteries, the "gathering," again was celebrated in Athens. The sacred objects of the cult, representing the presence of the goddess, were brought in procession from Eleusis to Athens on the first day of the celebration. On the second day the magistrate of Athens presided over a quasi-political convocation of the participants. The next two days consisted of purification rites, sacrifices, and a day of rest held in honor of Asclepius who, according to tradition, had arrived late for the ceremonies. (As it would be awkward to refuse a god initiation, Asclepius's lateness provided a precedent for late arrivals from afar.)

These rites, like those of the Lesser Mysteries, recognized Athenian political domination. But Athens was more than the site of government. To the participants in the Mysteries, this cosmopolitan center represented the Greek world in its homelessness; for although the goddess might visit Athens from time to time, she was at home only in Eleusis. All who would be initiated must come to Eleusis, for it was there that Demeter's own wandering had come to an end.

The participants were now ready to return home with the goddess. On the fifth day, the procession of priests and priestesses, officials and witnesses, and sponsors and participants wound along the

ancient *Sacred Way* from Athens to Eleusis. In contrast to the sorrow-
ful wandering of the goddess, this pilgrimage was a festive, joyful
occasion, jubilantly led by the bearers of flaming torches. After all,
the goddess had first walked these steps on behalf of the pilgrims,
who consequently had certain knowledge of the goal of their own
wandering. In his comedy *The Frogs*, the fifth-century B.C.E. Athenian playwright Aristophanes captured the flavor of this joyful procession, which was preceded by Iacchos, the jubilant deity of life:

> Let flames fly as the torch tosses in hand's hold
> Iacchos o Iacchos
> star of fire in the high rites of the night time.
> And the field shines in the torch light,
> and the old men's knees are limber,
> and they shake off aches and miseries
> and the years of their antiquity drop from them
> in the magical measure.
> Oh, torch-in-hand shining.
> Iacchos go before us to the marsh flowers and the meadow
> and the blest revel of dances.[8]

By the end of the day the participants, like Demeter, arrived at the
Kallichoron Well, where they spent the remainder of the evening
dancing and singing in praise of the goddess.

The sixth day was one of fasting and rest, again following the
example of the goddess. Found resting by the side of the Kallichoron
Well, she had been invited into the royal home by members of the
ruling family. Although she continued her fast, she accepted the hospitality of this royal home by drinking the *kykeon*, a "mixture" of
"meal and water with soft mint." Consequently, the pilgrims most
probably broke their own fast with this sacred drink. This drink was
offered by the priest, who was a descendent of Eumolpus, one of
those who had originally shown hospitality to Demeter in Eleusis and
to whom she had first shown her Mysteries. The initiates would now
be invited to enter into the *temenos,* the sacred precincts of Demeter
at Eleusis.

The topography of the sacred site itself imaged the course of
initiation. The Eleusinian hill by the Aegean upon which the sanctuary was built suggests the sacred mountain of traditional cosmology,
the link with the world of the gods above and below. Upon entering
the gates of the precinct, to their right the pilgrims encountered the

Ploutonion, a grotto in the hillside. In the sacred geography of Eleusis, this grotto represented the entrance to the underworld. Here then, at the point of union of the heavens, the earth, and the underworld, the joining of the sea and the plains, was the sacred site of Eleusis.

The initiation occurred just beyond the Ploutonion in the Telesterion, whose northwest corner was chiseled into the rock of the Eleusinian hill. Initiation must have involved the ritual epiphany of Demeter, the goddess shedding her disguise, even as she had before Metaneira, the earthly queen. Before Demeter's epiphany, according to the *Homeric Hymn,* Metaneira had voiced the Greek understanding of fated human existence: "Yet we mortals bear perforce what the gods send us, though we be grieved; for a yoke is set upon our necks" (lines 216–217). In her prototypical epiphany to Metaneira—and to all humans—Demeter echoed this perception: "Witless you mortals and dull to foresee your lot, whether of good or evil, that comes upon you" (lines 256–57). In the Hellenistic age, these words could only have been heard as a description of Tyche/Fortuna's capricious rule.

After the night of initiation there followed two days of rest and of rituals for the dead. On the ninth day, the new initiates returned from the center of the religious world to its cosmopolitan center in Athens, newly at home with the goddess. And like the goddess on the tenth day of her wandering, they knew the truth of her providential rule over the cosmopolitan world.

The Mystery Initiation

The meaning of the Eleusinian Mysteries is often named as one of the best kept secrets of history. It has often been interpreted as an agricultural myth in which the Corn Goddess alternately withholds and guarantees the fertility of the earth. The mythic cycle of Persephone, the Corn Maiden, parallels the annual cycle of the grain. For two-thirds of the year, corresponding to the times in which the fields of the Thriasian Plain are fertile, the Corn Maiden may be with her mother, Demeter. But for the remaining one-third of the year, from June to October, when the sun-scorched fields of Greece are barren and the seed grain is stored in subterranean silos, the Corn Maiden is with Hades, the Lord of the Underworld.[9] This interpretation assumes that the agricultural meaning of the myth later evolved an allegorical significance in which the annual sprouting of the new crop is taken as a symbol of eternal life.[10] Examples of this kind of agrarian allegory are familiar from early Christianity:

> Truly, truly, I say to you, unless a grain of wheat falls into the earth and dies, it remains alone; but if it dies, it bears much fruit.
>
> John 12:24

> What you sow does not come to life unless it dies.
>
> I Cor. 15:36

Thus, the third-century c.e. Christian apologist Hippolytus suggested that the highest grade of initiation at Eleusis consisted of showing the initiates "an ear of corn in silence reaped" (*Haer.* V, 3).

The *Homeric Hymn to Demeter,* however, suggests that the meaning of the Mysteries is not a later development of agrarian allegory but was in fact inseparable from agrarian imagery from the beginning. Demeter first showed her Mysteries to the Eleusinians immediately upon her restoration of fertility to the earth:

> And rich-crowned Demeter . . . straightway made fruit to spring up from the rich lands, so that the whole wide earth was laden with leaves and flowers. Then she went, and to the kings who deal justice, Triptolemus and Diocles, the horse-driver, and to doughty Eumolpus and Celeus, leader of the people, she showed the conduct of her rites and taught them all her mysteries.
>
> *Hymn Hom. Cer.* 470–476

The *Hymn* does not present agriculture as a natural process to be allegorized, but as human activity surrounded by divine guarantees.[11]

Something of the initiation itself is suggested by the *Homeric Hymn.* In what is perhaps its most often cited and well-known passage, the *Hymn* proclaims the initiate as "happy" (in Greek, *olbios*) (line 480), a designation that became formulaic in the Hellenistic world.[12] Most interpreters refer this "happiness" primarily to the afterlife. The Greeks, however, were not much concerned with the afterlife. In fact, Homer always used the same word to refer to worldly goods. Therefore, it would seem that the Eleusinian initiates' happiness embraced a transformed terrestrial mode of life.

Olbios, however, implies more than worldly prosperity. Initiatory happiness also is a valuation by the Eleusinian goddess of the agrarian life through participation in her share of "divine honor." Honor, a major theme of the *Hymn,* is a cosmic characteristic of the immortals. Plouton's honor is his rule of a third share of the cosmos (lines 85–87). It is his prerogative to distribute honor to others from his own share (lines 334–366), as it is also that of his brother Zeus (lines 441–447)—and indeed, that of "all the blessed and eternal gods" (lines 325–328). In the *Hymn,* Demeter, as "the greatest help and cause of joy" for both mortals and immortals, claims for herself a share of this honor (lines 268–269). By withdrawing from the company of gods and subsequently devastating the earth through famine (lines 301–313), she effectively robs the Olympians of their rightful honor (lines 311–313, 351–354). In response, Zeus promises both Demeter and Persephone whatever share of honor they might choose from among the immortals (lines 441–447, 459, 462).[13]

Demophoon is the only mortal in the *Hymn* to share in this divine honor. Accepting the hospitality of the Eleusinians during her quest for Persephone, Demeter attempts to show her gratitude and at the same time adopt a substitute for her abducted daughter by investing Demophoon with immortality, the quality of the divine company she had spurned. However, this gift of the goddess was destined to fail because the realms of the immortals and of the mortals belong to different levels of existence:

> I would have made your dear son deathless and unaging all his days and would have bestowed on him everlasting honour, but now he can in no way escape death and the fates. Yet shall unfailing honour always rest upon him, because he lay upon my knees and slept in my arms.   *Hymn Hom. Cer.* 260–264

Although in the Greek order of things it was not possible for even a goddess to bestow immortality upon a mortal, she could bestow her honor upon Demophoon—and upon all the children of Eleusis. It would seem, therefore, that Demophoon, who had lain upon Demeter's knees and slept in her arms, was the first of Demeter's initiates at Eleusis, before her epiphany to the house of Celeus (lines 268–283), and before she revealed her Mysteries to the Eleusinians.

The account of the transformation of Demophoon structurally parallels and complements that of the transformation of Persephone. Demophoon and Persephone are both transformed—initiated out of childhood—by a representative of the contrasexual and contra-elemental principle, and in each case, to the great horror of their mothers. Demophoon, the masculine principle, approached immortality through immersion in fire, the masculine element of Aristotelian physics. The agency of his transformation is Demeter, the feminine principle, whose action superficially appears to Metaneira as malevolent. Similarly, Persephone, the feminine principle, is made immortal through descent into the underworld (immersion in earth), the chthonic or feminine element. The agency of her transformation is Hades, the masculine principle, whose action likewise appears to Demeter as malevolent. In the transformative initiation, the maternal feminine as the source of life must nevertheless be transcended, through the transforming element, fire, which was so prominently present in Eleusinian iconography.

Eleusis and Athens

Eleusis was almost certainly annexed into the larger Athenian state of Attica for economic reasons. Greek cities were expected to feed themselves from grain grown on their own territories, an increasingly difficult task given the growth in urban population during the seventh and sixth centuries B.C.E.[14] Despite Attica's claim to be the original home of agriculture in addition to civilization and law,[15] and despite Plato's assertion that Attica was the first to produce an abundance of grain and barley,[16] this region was unable to feed its own population.[17] More than any other Greek city, Athens relied upon imported grain.[18] Strategically, this situation placed Athens at the mercy of any other power able to interrupt its supply.[19] In the early sixth century, according to Plutarch, this economic situation prompted Solon to ban the export of all agricultural products except for the plentiful olives and their oil (*Vit. Sol.*, 24),[20] for which the acid soil of Attica was especially well suited.[21] As barley was grown in the relatively poorer soil of the nearby Marathon and Mesogeia plains, the domestic supply of wheat in Attica was grown almost entirely in the Eleusinian Thriasian Plain, some of the most fertile land in Attica.[22]

Whether the *Homeric Hymn to Demeter* dates from before the Athenian domination of Eleusis, as most commentators think,[23] or was a response to Athenian domination, as some think,[24] scholars agree that the *Hymn* is non-Athenian and represents an Eleusinian discourse.[25] The *Hymn* thus presents an Eleusinian rural discourse as an alternative to that of Athenian urban civilization. Although civilization in antiquity was most often identified with "citification," from which the word is derived,[26] the *Hymn* implies an identification of civilization with the spread of cultivation (lines 468–469, 488–489). That identification was later made explicit with the introduction into

Eleusinian discourse of an agrarian mission to the nations by Triptolemus.[27] Eleusinian discourse thus established the rural and agrarian life as a value in itself over against urban dominance and exploitation.[28] This valuation of the rural life was expressed in cult through a ritual initiation into a share of the Eleusinian goddess' honor, and thus into a secure happiness sustained in the face of Athenian politico-economic domination. The well-known Eleusinian icon of wheat can thus be understood as a religio-economic emblem of agrarian identity and power, especially potent in face of Hellenistic urbanization. Its annual display was a religio-political gesture of autonomy and independence. Despite the later expansion of Hellenistic cosmopolitanism and then of the Roman Empire,[29] and despite the Ptolemaic cosmological revolution, the Eleusinian initiates never relinquished their grasp on the land and their belief in the values of the rural life.[30]

The Mysteries of Isis

Whereas Alexander's ideal of empire unified by a Greek culture was primarily realized in the cities of his former empire, a growing resistance to Hellenism began to characterize some urban centers by the second century B.C.E.[31] This urban resistance to Greek culture established the condition for a spread of native cults that were adapted, nevertheless, to a Hellenic model of mystery. The Mysteries of Isis provides the major example for these non-Hellenic Mysteries.

The Egyptian Isis was well-known outside her homeland since the fifth-century B.C.E. travelogues of Herodotus, which had identified her with Demeter (Book 2, 42; 48; 145). By the end of the fourth century B.C.E. she was already honored in the Athenian port of Piraeus among the Egyptians who had settled there.[32] The Hellenistic Mysteries of Isis eventually became a universal cult, recognizing no racial or geographic distinctions,[33] and were witnessed by "practically the entire inhabited world" (*Diod. Sic.* I, 25, 4). Like the Mysteries of Demeter, the cult of Isis survived until the imperial prohibition of paganism at the end of the fourth century C.E. In one sense, however, Isis survived even Christian dominance, for together with her divine son Horus, she is remembered in the sentiment and iconography of Roman Catholic Mariology.[34]

Isis came to be widely worshipped throughout the Hellenistic world largely because of patronage by Ptolemy I Soter. With the death of Alexander and the dissolution of his empire, Ptolemy, one of his Macedonian generals, secured his own rule over Egypt in 304. As part of his administration, he officially sanctioned the worship of Sarapis as the Hellenistic consort of Isis and established the cult's center in Alexandria.

According to one tradition reported in the late first century C.E. by both Plutarch (*De Is. et Os.* 28) and Tacitus (*Hist.* 4, 83–84), Ptolemy dreamed of a colossal statue of Pluto that was at Sinope in Pontus. In the dream, the statue commanded Ptolemy to bring it immediately to Alexandria. When Ptolemy had installed the statue there, "not without the help of divine providence," it was revealed to be that of "none other of the gods but Sarapis." As Plutarch concluded his report:

> It is better to identify Osiris with Dionysus and Sarapis with Osiris, who received this appellation at the time when he changed his nature. For this reason Sarapis is a god of all peoples in common, even as Osiris is; and this they who have participated in the holy rites well know.   *De Is. et Os.* 28

Whatever the historical origins of Sarapis,[35] this Hellenistic deity combined traits of the traditional Egyptian Osiris and of Apis, the "Osirified" or mummified and entombed sacred bull worshipped in Memphis, with those of the Greek Pluto (Hades) and Dionysus.[36] As such, this new Hellenized champion over fate provided for the spiritual needs of Ptolemy's new kingdom, which included both Egyptian and Greek citizens.

During the second and first centuries B.C.E., the worship of Isis and Sarapis spread rapidly from the famous Sarapeum at Alexandria throughout the Hellenistic world, carried by merchants, travellers, and the military.[37] Although the worship of Sarapis was widespread, the citizens of the Hellenistic world remembered nevertheless his Egyptian origins as Osiris. And it was Osiris's consort, Isis, who most captured popular interest.[38]

The Myth of Isis and Osiris

The many elements of the myth of Isis and Osiris are scattered throughout the ancient Egyptian pyramid texts.[39] However, a synoptic myth, known in the Hellenistic era, is recorded by Plutarch in his famous treatise *On Isis and Osiris,* which, together with the account of Diodorus Siculus (Book I) (circa 60–30 B.C.E.) and Apuleius's *Metamorphoses,* are the most important sources for the Hellenistic Isis.

According to Plutarch's account (*De Is. et Os.* 12–19), the couple, Isis and Osiris, are the offspring of Cronos and Rhea, the Greek equivalents of the Egyptian earth god, Geb, and the sky goddess, Nut.[40] Isis and Osiris were sister and brother, consorting with each other in the womb. Similarly, Nephthys, the twin sister of Isis, became the wife of Set (Typhon), the twin brother of Osiris; there was thus an interrelated quaternity of sister and brother, consort and spouse.

Osiris was the hero of Egyptian myth, delivering

> the Egyptians from their destitute and brutish manner of living. This he did [like Triptolemus of Eleusis legend] by showing them the fruits of cultivation, by giving them laws, and by teaching them to honor the gods. Later he travelled over the whole earth civilizing it.
> *De Is. et Os.* 13[41]

Nevertheless, Isis was the more important of the two, even in myth. For while Osiris was away on his civilizing journeys, Isis ruled in his stead. As Diodorus put it, "after Osiris had established the affairs of Egypt," he "turned the supreme power over to Isis his wife" (*Diod. Sic.* I, 17, 3). And Plutarch says that during her reign, Osiris's wicked brother, Set, was reported to have "attempted nothing revolutionary because Isis . . . was vigilant and alert; but when he [Osiris] returned home Typhon [Set] contrived a treacherous plot against him" (*De Is. et Os.* 13). This strategy of Set suggests that Isis was considered, by Set (and Hellenistic accounts) at least, to be the more formidable of the ruling pair.

Upon the return of Osiris from his journeys, Set and his henchmen plotted his murder. At festivities in honor of Osiris's return, they "jestingly" promised a beautiful chest to whomever corresponded exactly to its measurements. When Osiris took his turn, those involved in the plot "slammed down the lid, which they fastened by nails from the outside and also by using molten lead. Then they carried the chest to the river and sent it on its way to the sea" (*De Is. et. Os.* 13).

After Isis learned of her consort's fate, she immediately went into mourning and "wandered everywhere" in search of her entombed husband. Informed by some children of what had happened, she later discovered that the chest had been "cast up by the sea near the land of Byblus and . . . the waves had gently set it down in the midst of a clump of heather" (*De Is. et Os.* 15). The foliage around the chest had grown into a great tree admired by the King of Byblus who had it cut for use as a pillar in his palace. Isis requested and received this pillar/ sarcophagus of Osiris, which she returned home to Egypt. Such a cult pillar was erected before all Isis temples and represented the completion of Isis's quest for and reunion with her consort.[42]

By chance, however, Set came upon the sarcophagus of Osiris and "recognizing the body, he divided it into fourteen parts and scattered them, each in a different place" (*De Is. et Os.* 18), thereby establishing mythic justification for the widespread shrines of the Isis cult. Once again, the goddess wandered the world in search of her consort until at last she found and reassembled the body, with the exception of its phallus. She made a replica of this crucial part which became identified in her cult with the sarcophagus pillar. Finally, Osiris returned from the other world of death in support of his son, Horus, who, with this transcendent aid, finally was able to overcome their ancient antagonist, Set.[43]

The two-fold murder of Osiris by Set: his casting of the entombed Osiris into the Nile and his dismemberment of Osiris, and Osiris's subsequent restoration to life by Isis—in annual ritual celebration, as well as in the sonship of the Horus-Pharoah—all allude to an agrarian dimension of the Isis-Osiris myth. In the Isis temple at Philae, the body of the dead Osiris was represented with corn stalks growing from it. A priest watered the stalks from a pitcher. The accompanying inscription read: "This is the form of him whom one may not name, Osiris of the mysteries, who springs from the returning waters."[44] Plutarch reports that Isis was identified with the earth (*De Is. et Os.* 32), "not all of it, but so much of it as the Nile covers" (*De Is. et Os.* 38). Correspondingly, Osiris was identified with the Nile, into which he had been cast by Set. As depicted in the Isis temple at Philae, Osiris annually united with and fertilized Earth-Isis. In these rites, Osiris was understood to be "the whole source and faculty creative of moisture" (*De Is. et Os.* 33) and thus the cause of generation and the substance of the life-producing seed. As patron of the cultivated grain and vine, which he had introduced to the civilized world, Osiris had been identified with Dionysus by the Greeks and was known to the Egyptians as the corn-god, who, like the corn, annually was threshed—dismembered by Set—only to return from the dead in the new crop.

Set, according to one Hellenistic tradition, was the sea "into which the Nile discharges its waters and is lost to view and dissipated" (*De Is. et Os.* 32). He personified formlessness and chaos, whether as desert or ocean, and so was identified with that which was contrary to the principle of fecundity and cultivation personified by Isis and Osiris.

In the Hellenistic world, Isis no longer was seen as the Egyptian elemental Mother Earth, recipient of the fecundating Osiris. Rather, she ascended from her Egyptian throne on the Nile bank to mount her Hellenistic lunar throne, from where she presided over her Mysteries as the universal "Mother of All Things," as the lunar Queen of Heaven (*Met.* XI, 5).

Although the appeal of Eleusinian Demeter was primarily to the rural folk, the Hellenistic attraction of Isis, the ancient goddess of life[45] and guarantor of cosmic order[46] might be characterized as that of an urban Demeter. Osiris is portrayed in Hellenistic sources as the founder of cities (*Diod. Sic.* I, 15, 1; 19, 7). He advanced "community life" by introducing fruits that are most easily cultivated (*Diod. Sic.* I, 20, 3). According to the Isis aretologies, hymns praising and reciting her virtues, the goddess also built cities (*Diod. Sic.* I, 17, 4) and established laws (*Diod. Sic.* I, 27, 3) that made possible the founding of cities (Maroneia aretology, lines 30–31).[47] And, according to Plutarch, she distributed effigies of Osiris among the cities (*De Is. et Os.* 18). In the Hellenistic world the shrines of Isis were established primarily in port cities and centers of commerce,[48] where, with the exception of Rome during the first century B.C.E. and early first century C.E.,[49] Isis appealed increasingly to an urban social and intellectual elite.[50]

The Rites of Isis

The Hellenistic worship of Isis, like that of Demeter, had its private as well as public face. As the first-century B.C.E. historian Diodorus Siculus wrote,

> the [Egyptian] priests, having received the exact facts about these matters [concerning Isis and Osiris] as a secret not to be divulged, are unwilling to give out the truth to the public, on the ground that perils overhang any men who disclose to the common crowd the secret knowledge about these gods.   *Diod. Sic.* I, 27, 6

To the uninitiated, however, the public ceremonies of these Mysteries, like those of Demeter, presented a ritual manifestation of the profound discontinuity between everyday existence, buffeted by fortune, and the promise of a blessed existence under the providential guidance and protection of the revealed power of *Tychē Agathē*, the good fortune, one of the early and persistent epithets of Isis.[51]

As with the Eleusinian Mysteries, the public presence of Isis included lavish processions in her honor, such as are described by Apuleius in the final book of his novel (*Met.* XI, 7–12). It included also popular familiarity with the story of Isis and Osiris, such as Plutarch's late first-century synoptic account. And, of course, it included such popular testimonials as Apuleius's novel with its apparently moralistic message: "Do not be an ass; the religious life under the protection of the great goddess is better." This promise is spoken by the goddess herself to Lucius and to all readers of Apuleius's novel:

> Thou shalt live blessed in this world, thou shalt live glorious by my guide and protection, and when after thine allotted space of life thou descendest to hell, there thou shall see me in that subterranean firmament shining. . . . And if I perceive that thou art obedient to my commandment and addict to my religion, meriting by thy constant chastity my divine grace, know thou that I alone may prolong thy days above the time that the fates have appointed and ordained.
>
> *Met.* XI, 6

Apart from pietistic devotions in homes and private shrines, two types of public devotions were accorded Isis: daily rituals observed at her numerous shrines, and the annual celebrations of the Isiac liturgical year. The daily rituals consisted of prayer at the beginning of the day and in the afternoon. During midday, the shrines were open for private prayer and meditation. Accompanied by the joyful chanting of her devotees, they were closed at the end of the day.[52] The two major annual celebrations of the Isiac liturgical year were the fall Festival of Search and Discovery and the spring *Navigium Isidis*.

The Festival of Search and Discovery recalled the search of the grieving Isis for Osiris, whose discovery and subsequent resurrection were the occasions for public joy.[53] This theme of grievous wandering and joyous discovery provides the overall structure for Apuleius's novel.

Lucius received his long-sought antidotal rose from a priest of Isis during the second major Isiac festival, the *Navigium Isidis,* a celebration that "is dedicate to my [Isis's] service by an eternal religion" (*Met.* XI, 5).[54] A description of this elaborate, carnival-like festival is preserved in Apuleius's account of its celebration at Cenchraea, the port of Corinth. The reborn Lucius joined with the followers of Isis in their procession to the sea, to the same spot where the ass Lucius had encountered the goddess the night before, and from where the ship of Isis was to be launched.

The celebration of the *Navigium Isidis* had two meanings. The initiates' procession to the sea recalled Isis's wandering to the shores of Byblus in search for Osiris; simultaneously, it recalled Isis searching the Nile for her dismembered consort. As such, the procession ritualized human wandering over the "sea of life"[55] and anticipated the fall Festival of Search and Discovery. Second, the festival celebrated the spring calming of the rough winter seas. As Isis explains, "my priests and ministers do accustom, after the wintry and stormy tempests of the sea be ceased and the billows of his waves are still, to offer in my name a new ship, as a first-fruit of their navigation" (*Met.* XI, 5).

The launching of the ship of Isis was not only the celebration of renewed navigation but also a missionary symbol. Not bound like Demeter to a specific locale, Isis reached out to the periphery of the Hellenistic world on the life-giving waters of the Nile, which flowed into and transformed the Mediterranean world.[56] Elements of this important festival are preserved in popular Christianity to the present day.[57]

After launching the ship of Isis, Lucius returned to the temple of Isis where he was acclaimed "as a man raised from death to life" (*Met.* XI, 18) and where he declared his desire to be initiated into the Mysteries of Isis.

The Mysteries of Isis

The Mysteries of Isis, as they were called by the Greeks, were a Hellenistic development in the long history of the cult[58] and were apparently fashioned after the example of the Eleusinian Demeter, with whom the Greeks identified her. According to Plutarch's account of their origin, Ptolemy of Egypt was assisted in his Sarapis project by Timotheus of the priestly Eumolpid family from Eleusis, who had been invited to Egypt for the occasion (*De Is. et Os.* 28). In any case, the similarities between the *Homeric Hymn of Demeter* and the Hellenistic myth of Isis as narrated by Plutarch is a clear example of the shaping of non-Greek myth by religious conventions more familiar to a Hellenized cosmopolitanism.

According to Plutarch, the Mysteries of Isis, like those of Demeter, were founded by the goddess herself to immortalize her struggles:

> But the avenger, the sister and wife of Osiris, after she had quenched and suppressed the madness and fury of Typhon, was not indifferent to the contests and struggles which she had endured, nor to her own wanderings nor to her manifold deeds of wisdom and many feats of bravery, nor would she accept oblivion and silence for them, but she intermingled in the most holy rites portrayals and suggestions and representations of her experiences at that time, and sanctified them, both as a lesson in godliness and an encouragement for men and women who find themselves in the clutch of like calamities. *De Is. et Os.* 27

Further, according to Plutarch, when the wandering Isis came to Byblus in search of her consort, she rested by a spring in silence, speaking to no one but the maidservants of the Queen of Byblus. Impressed by the hairdressing and fragrance of this strange woman, the Queen sent for Isis, took her into her home, and employed her as the nurse for her infant. The scene is strikingly similar to Demeter's "initiation" of Demophoon:

> They relate that Isis nursed the child by giving it her finger to suck instead of her breast, and in the night she would burn away the mortal portions of its body. She herself would turn into a swallow and flit about the pillar [the sarcophagus of Osiris] with a wailing lament, until the queen who had been watching, when she saw her babe on fire, gave forth a loud cry and thus deprived it of immortality. Then the goddess disclosed herself. *De Is. et Os.* 16

The myths of both Demeter and the Hellenistic Isis exhibit similar motifs: the goddess wandering in quest of familial completion, the heavenly queen coming to a terrestrial at-homeness in an earthly queen's palace, the confrontation of the unrecognized goddess by the horrified mother resulting in her son's loss of immortality, the epiphany of the goddess, the restoration of the lost family member, and the final establishment of her celestial home. Thus, the Mysteries of Isis,

like those of Demeter, rested on the Hellenistic perception that existence, like the goddess herself, might be transformed from local or
regional alienation into cosmopolitan at-homeness.

Despite his insistence on keeping secret "what was said and
done" at Lucius's initiation (*Met.* XI, 23), Apuleius continues to
present much of what is known of initiation into the Mysteries of Isis.
To her initiates, Isis promised, as she did to the transformed Lucius,
that

> thou shalt return again to be a man. Thou shalt live blessed in this
> world, thou shalt live glorious by my guide and protection, and
> when after thine allotted space of life thou descendest to hell, there
> thou shalt see me in that subterranean firmament shining (as thou
> seest me now).   *Met.* XI, 6

Those who desired initiation into the Mysteries of Isis had to
await her summons (*Met.* XI, 19). As Isis's purposes were communicated most often through dreams,[59] her invitation was sought
through the traditional technique of incubation. Initiates engaged a
room within the temple complex where they devoted themselves to
the daily practice of temple rituals (*Met.* XI, 20), observed dietary
restrictions, and received preparatory instruction (*Met.* XI, 21).
When the invitational dream occurred, a priest was assigned to guide
the suppliant through the initiation.

The priest's task was to interpret "such things as were necessary
to the use and preparation" of the initiate. This catechism was preserved in sacred books written in Egyptian hieroglyphics, a language
"impossible to be read" by profane noninitiates (*Met.* XI, 22).[60]
Following purification by baptism and ten days of fasting, noninitiates
were excluded from the temple, and the prospective initiate, secluded
from the profane eyes of the curious, was invested with a new linen
robe and led to the "most secret and sacred part of the temple" (*Met.*
XI, 23). Here, Apuleius, in a famous passage, has Lucius describe
how

> I approached near unto hell, even to the gates of Proserpine
> [Persephone], and after that I was ravished throughout all the ele-
> ments, I returned to my proper place: about midnight I saw the sun
> brightly shine, I saw likewise the gods celestial and the gods infernal,
> before whom I presented myself and worshipped them.
>   *Met.* XI, 23

Through this "voluntary death and a difficult recovery to health" (*Met.* XI, 21), the initiate finally was freed from the "maze of miserable wanderings" in which he had been entangled by fortune (*Met.* XI, 20) and was able to return home (*Met.* XI, 24) to his friends and parents (*Met.* XI, 26)—acknowledging now, however, the priest of Isis as his spiritual Father (*Met.* XI, 26) and the universal goddess herself, who nourishes all the world, as his loving Mother (*Met.* XI, 25).

The Universal Goddess

The sovereignty of the universal goddess in the Hellenistic world can be illustrated not only by the Greek Demeter and the Egyptian Isis, but also by two other deities: the Syrian goddess Atargatis, and the Phrygian goddess Cybele.

The Syrian Goddess

Atargatis, the Syrian Goddess, was related to other Near Eastern mother goddesses such as the Babylonian and Assyrian goddess Ishtar, and the Phoenician goddess Astarte. Her consort was the fertility god Hadad (Tammuz and Baal, respectively). Her worship, spread largely by Syrian slaves and merchants, extended from her center at Hieropolis in northern Syria into Egypt and Greece by the third century B.C.E., and then into Italy and the West. Her Mysteries were celebrated in the Peloponnesian town of Thuria.[61] The two major sources for her worship are a treatise, *On the Syrian Goddess,* by Lucian of Samasata, the second-century C.E. writer and satirist of Syrian birth, and Apuleius's *Metamorphoses,* which presents a colorful if unsympathetic account of Lucius's treatment as an ass in the service of a wandering band of the goddess' priests (*Met.* VIII, 24–30).

Although Atargatis is one of the divine characters of Apuleius's novel, shares characteristics with them, and is identified in other contexts with Isis,[62] she is not identified with the company of goddesses in this novel, but is mocked. Apparently, Atargatis is excluded from Apuleius's particular configuration of sympathetic relationships established with Isis precisely because of her association, in the fictive world of Apuleius's novel, with Lucius's ill-fortune. The ass introduced the account of his ritual service to Philebus, a priest of the Syrian Goddess, with the observation that

> my evil fortune, which was ever so cruel against me, whom I, by travel of so many countries, could in no wise escape nor appease the envy thereof by all the woes I had undergone, did more and more cast its blind and evil eyes upon me, with the intervention of new means to afflict my poor body, in giving me another master very fit for my hard fate.   *Met.* VIII, 24

Lucian's description of the image of Atargatis in her temple at Hieropolis is nevertheless similar to Apuleius's description of Isis's composite nature (*Met.* XI, 2). Lucian wrote that in the Greek idiom, she "is certainly Hera, but she also has something of Athena, Aphrodite, Selene, Rhea, Artemis, Nemesis and the Fates" (*Syr. D.* 32).[63] Because Lucian interpreted the image of Atargatis's consort as Zeus, Atargatis was "undoubtedly" Zeus's spouse, Hera. By extension, she was equated as well with the ancient Greek Earth Mother, Rhea, and also with Athena, who had sprung fullborn from the head of Zeus. Specifically, the Hieropolitan image of Atargatis wore a girdle "with which," according to Lucian, "they adorn only celestial Aphrodite" (*Syr. D.* 32). Aphrodite presided over fertility in a manner strikingly reminiscent of the Eleusinian Mysteries. She had entrusted her dead consort, Adonis, to Persephone, but the Queen of the Underworld refused to restore him until Zeus decreed that he must spend a portion of the year in the underworld with her and the remainder of the year with Aphrodite. Nemesis, who had fled the amorous advances of Zeus by assuming various nonhuman forms, especially that of a fish, reminded Lucian that although the image of Atargatis at Hieropolis was of a complete woman, he had seen

> a likeness of Derkete [Atargatis] in Phoenicia, a strange sight! It is a woman for half its length, but from the thighs to the tips of the feet a fish's tail stretches out . . . [for] they consider fish something sacred.   *Syr. D.* 14

The rays surrounding the head of Atargatis suggested to Lucian her celestial quality as Selene, the Greek moon goddess, a lunar nature associated also with Artemis and Nemesis. Like Tyche and her classical predecessors, the Fates, Atargatis wore a turreted crown and carried, like Artemis, the distaff, a staff for holding flax or wool used in spinning—an image of feminine tasks but also of the feminine web of fate. Like Isis, the lunar Queen Atargatis was able to overcome the capricious rule of Tyche.

The Great Mother of the Gods

The worship of Cybele, the Great Mother of the Gods, spread from its chief sanctuary, Pessinus in Phrygia, to Greece by the early fourth century B.C.E., and then on to Egypt and Italy. Heeding the counsel of the Sibylline oracle concerning the threat of foreign invaders, the Roman senate brought her worship to Rome in 214 B.C.E. as the first officially sanctioned Eastern cult. By the end of the Republic in 31 B.C.E., worship of the *Magna Mater* in the Roman world rivaled that of Isis in importance.

Cybele had been identified by the Greeks with Rhea and, independent of her consort Attis, with Demeter. The Romans also associated her with Ceres (Demeter), but as a Near Eastern goddess she was most closely associated with Atargatis. Lucian even records a tradition—the authenticity of which he was dubious—in which Attis was the founder of the Hieropolitan temple of Atargatis/Cybele/Rhea (*Syr. D.* 15).

Apuleius vividly described the painted and elaborately robed bands of Galli, eunuch servants of Atargatis and Cybele, who wandered from place to place with an image of the goddess borne by an ass, dancing and whirling to the music of shrill Syrian pipes (*Met.* VIII; also referred to by Lucian, *Syr. D.* 43). As crowds gathered, they would cut their arms with the swords and axes they carried, and flog themselves with scourges. In response to their ecstatic performances and resulting divinations, the excited crowds would offer money and food to the goddess through her servants (*Met.* VIII, 27–29). Lucian reported this same orgy of blood-drawing and lashing as preparatory to a practice of castration (*Syr. D.* 50).

The account of Attis's death by bleeding following his self-mutilation in service to the goddess provided the mythic paradigm for the ritual castration that characterized the worship of both Atargatis and Cybele. This ecstatic ceremony of emasculation is vividly described by Lucian:

> While the rest [of the Galli] are playing flutes and performing the rites, frenzy comes upon many, and many who have come simply to watch subsequently perform this act. I will describe what they do.

> The youth for whom these things lie in store throws off his clothes, rushes to the center with a great shout, and takes up a sword, which, I believe, has stood there for this purpose for many years. He grabs it and immediately castrates himself. Then he rushes through the city holding in his hands the parts he has cut off. He takes female clothing and women's adornment from whatever house he throws these parts into. This is what they do at the Castration.
>
> *Syr. D.* 51

Having fallen into a frenzy climaxed by their self-mutilation, the Galli became eunuch servants of Atargatis and Cybele, "feminine" in their service to the Great Mother. Their transformation was signified by the wearing of women's clothing, performing traditionally female tasks (*Syr. D.* 27), and by referring to one another in the feminine gender (*Met.* VIII, 26).

As the once localized goddesses, originating from Greece, Egypt, Syria, and Phrygia, emerged from their regional origins to become international deities in the Hellenistic world, they became sympathetically associated with one another through their common antithesis to the rule of Tyche/Fortuna. This process of cultural interaction was not accidental or arbitrary. Rather, deities of different historical origin came to participate in the common structures and concerns of an internationalized and universalized Hellenistic cultural system. The principle of feminine resemblance organized the seemingly diverse structures of early Hellenistic syncretism and gave coherence and meaning to its play of existential antipathy and soteriological sympathy.

Notes

1. See, for instance, George E. Mylonas, *Eleusis and the Eleusinian Mysteries* (Princeton, N.J.: Princeton University Press, 1961), p. 261.

2. S. Angus, *The Mystery-Religions: A Study in the Religious Background of Early Christianity,* 2nd ed. (New York: Dover, 1975), pp. 76–77.

3. The Hellenistic revival of the Eleusinian Mysteries is indicated by expansions of the sanctuary during this period. See Mylonas, chaps. VI and VII.

4. Mylonas, p. 3.

5. Martin P. Nilsson, *Greek Folk Religion* (New York: Harper, 1961), pp. 26–30.

6. See *Apollodorus* II, 5, 13, 2–3; *Diod. Sic.* IV, 25, 14.

7. Nilsson, pp. 24–26. The following summary of the Eleusinian Mystery calendar follows that of Mylonas, chap. IX.

8. Aristophanes, *The Frogs,* trans. Richard Lattimore (New York: New American Library, 1970), p. 43.

9. Nilsson, pp. 50–54.

10. Nilsson, p. 63.

11. Larry Alderink, "Mythic and Cosmological Structures in the Homeric Hymn to Demeter," *Numen* XXIX, 1 (1982), p. 8.

12. Nilsson, pp. 58–59.

13. Persephone received honor only during the four months she was in the underworld, that is, a third of her husband's third share of honor.

14. John V. A. Fine, *The Ancient Greeks* (Cambridge, Mass.: Harvard University Press, 1983), p. 94.

15. Mylonas, p. 21.

16. *Menexenos* 7; cited by Mylonas, p. 21.

17. Augustus Boeckh, *The Public Economy of the Athenians,* 2nd German ed., trans. Anthony Lamb (Boston: Little, Brown, 1857), p. 109; Humphrey Michel, *The Economics of Ancient Greece,* 2nd ed. (New York: Barnes and Noble, 1957), p. 48.

18. G. E. M. de Ste. Croix, *The Origins of the Peloponnesian War* (Ithaca, N.Y.: Cornell University Press, 1972), p. 46.

19. Ste. Croix, p. 47.

20. J. B. Bury and Russell Meiggs, *A History of Greece,* 4th ed. (New York: St. Martin's Press, 1975), p. 122.

21. N. G. L. Hammand, *A History of Greece to 322* B.C., 2nd ed. (Oxford: Clarendon Press, 1967), p. 12.

22. Pausanias (I, 38, 6) claimed that the Eleusinian Plains were the first to bear grain. See also Margaret O. Wason, *Class Struggles in Ancient Greece* (New York: Howard Fertig, 1973), p. 77.

23. See T. W. Allen, W. R. Halliday, and E. E. Sikes, *The Homeric Hymns,* 2nd ed. (Oxford: Clarendon Press, 1936), p. 113; and N. J. Richardson (ed.), *The Homeric Hymn to Demeter* (Oxford: Clarendon Press, 1974), pp. 6–11.

24. Francis R. Walton, "Athens, Eleusis, and the Homeric Hymn to Demeter," *Harvard Theological Review* 45 (1952), pp. 105–114.

25. See especially Allen and Halliday, p. 113.

26. G. E. M. de Ste. Croix, *Class Struggle in the Ancient Greek World* (Ithaca, N.Y.: Cornell University Press, 1981), pp. 10–11.

27. The legend of Triptolemus had entered Eleusis discourse by the sixth century. See Mylonas, p. 20; C. Kerényi, *Eleusis, Archetypal Image of Mother and Daughter,* trans. Ralph Manheim (New York: Pantheon Books, 1967), p. 125. The relation of the explicit linking of civilization to cultivation by Osiris as reported by Plutarch (*De Is. et Os.* 13) to the mission of Triptolemus has not been fully explored. See Theodor Hopfner, *Ueber Isis*

und Osiris, vol. 1 (Darmstadt, Germany: Wissenschaftlich Buchgesellschaft, 1967), p. 35.

28. Ste. Croix, *Class Struggle,* pp. 10–11.

29. Marcus Aurelius, Commodus, and L. Verus, the well-known Roman emperors who were initiated into the Eleusinian Mysteries, represented a late Stoic valuing of rural retreat as a technique whereby nature helps put one in contact with oneself. See, for example, Marcus Aurelius's *Meditations* 4, 3.

30. Agrarian life, structured around remains from the ancient Sanctuary of Demeter, persisted at Eleusis until modern industrialization. See Mylonas, chaps. I and II.

31. Kurt Rudolf, *Gnosis: The Nature and History of Gnosticism,* 2nd ed., trans. and ed. Robert McLachlan Wilson (San Francisco: Harper & Row, 1983), pp. 286, 288.

32. Sharon Kelly Heyob, *The Cult of Isis Among Women in the Graeco-Roman World* (Leiden: E. J. Brill, 1975), p. 6.

33. Harold R. Willoughby, *Pagan Regeneration: A Study of Mystery Initiations in the Graeco-Roman World* (Chicago: University of Chicago Press, 1974), p. 176.

34. Marina Warner, *Alone of All Her Sex: The Myth and the Cult of the Virgin Mary* (New York: Pocket Books, 1978), pp. 98, 193, 208–209, 266.

35. For a summary of views concerning the origin and dating of the Sarapis cult, see Heyob, pp. 2–6.

36. See also *Diod. Sic.* I, 25, 1–2.

37. On the spread of the Isis/Sarapis cult, see Willoughby, pp. 180–184; Thomas Allan Brady, *The Reception of the Egyptian Cults by the Greeks (330–30* B.C.) (Columbia, Mo.: University of Missouri, 1935); J. Gwyn Griffiths, *Plutarch's De Iside et Osiride* (University of Wales Press, 1970), pp. 41–42; Vera Frederika Vanderlip, *The Four Greek Hymns of Isidorus and the Cult of Isis,* American Studies in Papyrology 12 (Toronto: A. M. Hakkert, 1972), pp. 75–83; Heyob, pp. 6–36; and Robert A. Wild, "The Known Isis-Sarapis Sanctuaries of the Roman Period", *Aufstieg und Niedergang der Römischen Welt* II, 17; 4 (Berlin and New York: Walter de Gruyter, 1984), pp. 1739–1851.

38. Willoughby, p. 176.

39. Griffiths, pp. 33–36; Heyob, pp. 37–40; and Howard Clark Kee, *Miracle in the Early Christian World* (New Haven, Conn.: Yale University Press, 1983), pp. 105–108.

40. See also *Diod. Sic.,* I, 13, 4–5.

41. See also *Diod. Sic.* I, 14, 1 and 20, 3.

42. See also *Diod. Sic.* I, 22, 6–7.

43. See also *Diod. Sic.* I, 21.

44. Reported by James G. Frazer, *The Golden Bough, Part IV: Adonis, Attis, Osiris,* 3rd ed., vol. II (New York: Macmillan, 1914), pp. 89–90.

45. Heyob, p. 1.

46. Kee, pp. 108–119.
47. The Maroneia aretology is cited by Kee, p. 125.
48. Heyob, pp. 7–9; Kee, p. 127.
49. Heyob, pp. 18–36.
50. Kee, p. 131.
51. Vanderlip, pp. 31–32, 78, 94–96.
52. Willoughby, pp. 184–185.
53. Griffiths, p. 62–63; and Reginald E. Witt, *Isis in the Graeco-Roman World* (Ithaca, N.Y.: Cornell University Press, 1971), pp. 162, 180–181.
54. See Witt, chap. XIII.
55. Witt, p. 183.
56. Kee, p. 118.
57. Witt, pp. 183–184.
58. Griffiths, pp. 42–43; Heyob, p. 57.
59. J. Gwyn Griffiths, *Apuleius of Madauros: The Isis-Book (Metamorphoses, Book XI)* (Leiden: E. J. Brill, 1975), p. 279.
60. Griffiths, *Isis-Book,* p. 285.
61. N. G. L. Hammond and H. H. Scullard (eds.), *The Oxford Classical Dictionary,* 2nd ed. (Oxford: Clarendon Press, 1970), p. 136.
62. Vanderlip, p. 28, n. 18.
63. Harold W. Attridge and Robert A. Oden (eds.), *The Syrian Goddess (De Dea Syria)* (Missoula, Mont.: Scholars Press, 1976).

Selected Bibliography

The Mysteries

S. Angus, *The Mystery-Religions: A Study in the Religious Background of Early Christianity,* 2nd ed. (New York: Dover, 1975).
Ugo Bianchi, *The Greek Mysteries* (Leiden: E. J. Brill, 1976).
Franz Cumont, *Oriental Religions in Roman Paganism* (New York: Dover, 1956).
Joscelyn Godwin, *Mystery Religions in the Ancient World* (New York: Harper & Row, 1981), is an interpretation from the perspective of perennial philosophy.
Bruce M. Metzger, "A Classified Bibliography of the Graeco-Roman Mystery Religions 1924–1973, with a Supplement 1974–1977," *Aufstieg und Niedergang der Römischen Welt* II, 17. 3 (Berlin and New York: Walter de Gruyter, 1984), pp. 1259–1423.
Richard Reitzenstein, *Hellenistic Mystery-Religions: Their Basic Ideas and Significance,* trans. John E. Steely, (Pittsburgh, Pa.: Pickwick Press, 1978).

Harold R. Willoughby, *Pagan Regeneration: A Study of Mystery Initiations in the Greco-Roman World* (Chicago: University of Chicago Press, 1974).

The Homeric Hymn to Demeter

T. W. Allen, W. R. Halliday, and E. E. Sikes, *The Homeric Hymns,* 2nd ed. (Oxford: Clarendon Press, 1936).

Hesiod, The Homeric Hymns and Homerica, rev. ed., trans. Hugh G. Evelyn-White, in the Loeb Classical Library (Cambridge, Mass.: Harvard University Press, 1936).

N. J. Richardson (ed.), *The Homeric Hymn to Demeter* (Oxford: Clarendon Press, 1974).

The Eleusinian Mysteries

C. Kerényi, *Eleusis: Archetypal Image of Mother and Daughter,* trans. Ralph Manheim, in the Bollingen Series (New York: Pantheon, 1967).

George E. Mylonas, *Eleusis and the Eleusinian Mysteries* (Princeton, N.J.: Princeton University Press, 1961).

R. Gordon Wasson, Albert Hofmann, and Carl A. P. Ruck, *The Road to Eleusis: Unveiling the Secret of the Mysteries* (New York: Harcourt, 1978). The thesis of this work, that the Eleusinian Mysteries involved a hallucinogen derived from ergot, which grows on the local grain, should not be dismissed too quickly, given the acceptance of Wasson's thesis concerning the Soma ritual of Vedic India in *Soma: Divine Mushroom of Immortality* (New York: Harcourt, n.d.). In addition to a translation of *The Homeric Hymn to Demeter,* this short volume also includes translations of other ancient texts pertaining to the Eleusinian Mysteries.

The Myth of Isis and Osiris

J. Gwyn Griffiths (ed. and trans.), *Plutarch's De Iside et Osiride,* with commentary (University of Wales Press, 1970).

———, *Apuleius of Madauros: The Isis-Book (Metamorphoses Book XI)* (Leiden: E. J. Brill, 1975).

Plutarch, *De Iside et Osiride,* in *Moralia,* vol. v, trans. Frank C. Babbitt, in the Loeb Classical Library (Cambridge, Mass.: Harvard University Press, 1936).

Diodorus Siculus, *Library of History,* 12 vols., trans. C. H. Oldfather et al., in the Loeb Classical Library (Cambridge, Mass.: Harvard University Press, 1933–1957).

R. T. van der Paardt, *Apuleius Madaurensis, The Metamorphoses: A Com-*

mentary on Book III with Text and Introduction (Amsterdam: A. M. Hakkert, 1971).

Studies of Isis

Sharon Kelly Heyob, *The Cult of Women in the Graeco-Roman World* (Leiden: E. J. Brill, 1975).

Reinhold Merkelbach, *Roman und Mysterium in der Antike* (Munich and Berlin: C. H. Beck, 1962).

Friedrich Solmsen, *Isis Among the Greeks and Romans* (Cambridge, Mass.: Harvard University Press, 1979).

Reginald E. Witt, *Isis in the Greco-Roman World* (Ithaca, N.Y.: Cornell University Press, 1971).

The Syrian Goddess

Monika Hoerig, "Dea Syria—Atargatis," *Aufstieg und Niedergang der Römischen Welt* II, 17. 3 (Berlin and New York: Walter de Gruyter, 1984), pp. 1536–1581, includes a comprehensive bibliography.

Lucian, *The Goddess of Surrye*, vol. IV, trans. M. Harmon, in the Loeb Classical Library (Cambridge, Mass.: Harvard University Press, 1925). This translation imitates the fourteenth-century English of Sir John Mandeville in order to preserve Lucian's parody of the style of Heraclitus, which makes for very difficult reading.

———, *The Syrian Goddess* (*De Dea Syria*), trans. Harold W. Attridge and Robert A. Oden (Missoula, Mont.: Scholars Press, 1976).

Robert A. Oden, Jr., *Studies in Lucian's De Syria Dea* (Missoula, Mont.: Scholars Press, 1977).

Herbert A. Strong and John Garstang, *The Syrian Goddess* (London: Constable, 1913), includes a life of Lucian and a commentary on the text.

The Great Mother of the Gods

Grant Showerman, *The Great Mother of the Gods* (Madison, Wis.: Bulletin of the University of Wisconsin, 1901).

Garth Thomas, "Magna Mater and Attis", *Aufstieg und Niedergang der Römischen Welt* II, 17. 3 (Berlin and New York: Walter de Gruyter, 1984), pp. 1500–1535.

Maarten J. Vermaseren, *Cybele and Attis: The Myth and The Cult,* trans. A. M. H. Lemmers (London: Thames and Hudson, 1977).

4

Reformations and Innovations

The sociopolitical and cosmological transformations that character-ized the Hellenistic world established the conditions and structures for the adaptation of traditional regional piety, a revival of Hellenic Mysteries, and a Hellenistic shaping of non-Hellenistic cults of the goddess. Other traditional cults, such as those of Dionysus and Yah-weh, were also reformed to the Hellenistic cultural system, and new religions indigenous to Hellenistic structures, such as Mithraism and Christianity, were created.

REFORMATIONS

The Hellenistic reformation of Judaism was marked in part by a Jewish wisdom tradition with its theological speculations about So-phia, a female consort of Yahweh. This remarkable feminizing ten-dency within the most singularly patriarchal of ancient traditions dra-matically illustrates the sovereignty of the feminine principle over a Hellenistic religious system. By the second century C.E., however, Judaism was clearly reestablished as the patriarchal Judaism of the rabbis and retained little trace of its flirt with the feminine.

During this same period of late antiquity, the admission of men into what reportedly had been an exclusively female cult of Dionysus suggests a "masculinization" of this cult, dramatically different from its pre-Hellenistic form. The cult of Dionysus, the immanent, chthonic god of the Greeks, and that of Yahweh, the transcendent, celestial deity of the Jews, represent two radically different religious orientations. Yet in the Hellenistic period, these traditions could be compared with one another.

Dionysus

In his Dionysian drama, *The Bacchae* (407 B.C.E.), the tragedian Euripides had the blind seer Tiresias say:

> Mankind . . . possesses two supreme blessings. First of these is the goddess Demeter, or Earth—whichever name you choose to call her by. It was she who gave to man his nourishment of grain. But after her there came the son of Semele [Dionysus] who matched her present by inventing liquid wine as his gift to man.
>
> *Bacch.* 274–297[1]

Tiresias's pronouncement characterizes as well the succeeding Hellenistic age in which the Dionysian Mysteries, along with those of Demeter, were accorded international acclaim.

Since Herodotus, the Greek tradition had equated Dionysus with the Egyptian Osiris (*Hdt.* II. 144), an identification repeated in the Hellenistic period by Plutarch (*De Is. et Os.* 34), who further identified Dionysus/Osiris with Sarapis (*De. Is. et Os.* 28). But little is known about Dionysian practices in the Hellenistic age; and what is known, largely inferred from iconographic evidence, indicates a wide variety in the forms and expressions of his cult. There are, however, certain common themes that recur amidst the diversity of his Hellenistic worship to which the classical myth had already given expression.

The Myth of Dionysus

Dionysus was held to be the son of Zeus and the mortal woman Semele, daughter of Cadmus, King of Thebes (*Hymn Hom. Bacch.* I, VII, and XXVI). Encouraged by the jealousy of Hera, Semele contrived, like Psyche, to view fully the divinity of her lover and met with similar disastrous consequences. Unable to bear the full epiphany of Zeus's Olympian splendor, Semele was struck dead by his fiery radi-

ance. Nevertheless, Zeus stitched their unborn child to his thigh and
carried the fetus to its full term (*Diod. Sic.* III, 62, 1–IV, 5, 4). As
sung by the chorus of *The Bacchae:*

> So his mother bore him once
> in labor bitter; lightning-struck
> forced by fire that flared from Zeus,
> consumed, she died, untimely torn,
> in childbed dead by blow of light!
> Of light the son was born!
>
> Zeus it was who saved his son;
> with speed outrunning mortal eye,
> bore him to a private place,
> bound the boy with clasps of gold;
> in his thigh as in a womb,
> concealed his son from Hera's eyes.
>
> And when the weaving Fates fulfilled the time,
> the bull-horned god was born of Zeus.
>   *Bacch.* 88–101

Pursued by Hera, the young child was finally entrusted to the
nymphs of Nysa, who protected and raised him (*Hymn Hom. Bacch.*
XXVI). Dionysus discovered wine in Nysa, and as an adult he spread
this gift, together with his cult, throughout the world. His wanderings
took him from Thrace, his traditional place of origin, eastward (like
Alexander) to the shores of the Ganges, whence he returned to travel
throughout Greece. During his travels to Naxos, he was kidnapped
by pirates whom Dionysus turned into dolphins (*Hymn Hom. Bacch.*
VII). After retrieving his mother from the underworld (*Paus.* II, 20,
3; 22, 1; 23, 85; and 37, 5), he was finally received into the company
of the Olympian gods.

The early stories of Dionysus's mythic return from the East into
Greece and his subsequent acceptance into the Hellenistic world were
marked by a variety of adventures that tell of the widespread popular
acceptance of this "new" deity in the face of official rejection. Euripides's account in *The Bacchae* is exemplary.

The Bacchae is a story of conflict between Pentheus, the young
king of Thebes, and Dionysus. Although Dionysus is the son of Zeus,
god of order, Pentheus understands the spontaneous worship of this
"new" god as anarchical, a threat to the established order of things.
And although Dionysus insists that his female initiates remain chaste,

Pentheus can believe only that their nocturnal activities are sexually licentious. Pentheus's curiosity concerning the practices of this new cult, however, leads to his being mistaken for an animal of Dionysus by his frenzied followers, who, led by Pentheus's mother, tear the young king apart, just as the Thracian women, according to some accounts, had disposed of the young Dionysus.

The ready popular acceptance of Dionysus in the face of official rejection attests that Dionysus was not in fact a foreign deity who belatedly made his way into the Olympian pantheon after his wilder excesses had been curbed; rather, he represented an ancient chthonic sensibility that existed before the official cults with which he was still contrasted. He generally was depicted as an effeminate character, as Diodorus Siculus observed (IV, 4, 2), and his imagery contrasted sharply with the pronounced virility of heroic Olympian deities such as his father, Zeus, and his brother, Apollo. Stories of Dionysus's entry into Greece thus represented his homecoming, and his followers responded to the feminine principle of nature that he embodied and that was antithetical to the transcendent Olympians.[2]

Born of a mortal and divinely reborn, this wandering deity was the basis for a revival of the Dionysian cult in the Hellenistic age. His cult spread to Egypt and, from his influence in Magna Graecia, throughout Italy by the third century B.C.E. Introduced in Rome in 496 B.C.E., it was well known there by the second century B.C.E.[3]

The Mysteries of Dionysus

The cult of Dionysus belonged to the resurgence of the chthonic evocations of the sacred that characterized the Hellenistic age. Like the Mysteries of Isis, his Mysteries were primarily a Hellenistic development and differed from his classical orgies (in Greek, *orgia,* meaning sacred rites).[4] Participation in these older rites, as dramatized by Euripides, was limited to women,[5] although by the mid-third century B.C.E., participation in the cult was open to both men and women.[6] The Mysteries of this ancient deity of the theater apparently were not so veiled from the curiosity of the profane public as were those of Demeter.[7]

In order to keep the Bacchanalia, the festival of Dionysus or Bacchus as he was also known, an initiate had to become a *bacchus* (masc.) or a *bacchē* (fem.), one who is possessed or inspired by the god. As the old hymn to Dionysus quoted by Euripides in *The Bacchae* begins:

> Blessed, blessed are those who know the mysteries of god,
> Blessed is he who hallows his life in the worship of god,
> he whom the spirit of god possesseth, who is one
> with those who belong to the holy body of god.
>
> *Bacch.* 73–75

According to Euripides, the god in his animal form of bull, lion, goat, or fawn was sacrificed, torn apart by his followers, his warm flesh eaten and his fresh blood drunk. This mythic theme was ritualized in the biennial midwinter *oreibasia* or mountain-dancing festival, which concluded with the *ōmophagia* or tearing and eating of the theriomorphic deity. Whether this sacrifice was an actual or a ritualized act, or even a dramatic *mis en scène* of Euripides's tragedy, it signified an immediate partaking by the pious of life in its essence as embodied by the god.[8]

As the essence of life, Dionysus was associated not only with blood but also with ivy, berries, and oak and fir trees. His cult titles included "the Power in the Tree," "the Blossom-Bringer," "the Fruit-Bringer," and "the Abundance of Life."[9] In the Hellenistic period, Plutarch knew Dionysus as "the lord and master . . . of the nature of every sort of moisture," and in support of this understanding cited a passage from Pindar:

> May gladsome Dionysus swell the fruit upon the trees,
> The hallowed splendor of harvest-time.
>
> *De Is. et Os.* 35

To his followers Dionysus was *Lysios* (redeemer), one who was able to deliver or redeem them from everydayness, from an existence perceived as oppressive through an ecstatically revealed order grounded in the natural flow of life itself.

Wine emerged as the dominant Dionysian emblem for the fullness of life (*Diod. Sic.* III, 2–74 *passim*). As Dionysus was transformed into immortality, so wine is the enduring, transformed essence of the grape; it is of the same blood-red hue as the essence of animal life. These aspects of Dionysus were ritualized in the spring festival associated with the drinking of wine.

The presence of wine represented the presence of the god. In *The Bacchae*, for example, we read of the Maenads:

One woman struck her thyrsus against a rock and a fountain of cool
water came bubbling up. Another drove her fennel in the ground,
and where it struck the earth, at the touch of a god, a spring of wine
poured out.   *Bacch.* 702–707

Or again, the second century c.e. Greek traveller Pausanias reported
in his *Description of Greece* that in Elis,

three pots are brought into the building by the priests [of Dionysus]
and set down empty in the presence of the citizens and of any
strangers who may chance to be in the country. The doors of the
building are sealed by the priests themselves and by any others who
may be so inclined. On the morrow they are allowed to examine the
seals, and on going into the building they find the pots filled with
wine.   *Paus.* VI, 26, 1–2

This Dionysian wine ritual was incorporated into Christian imagery by the Gospel of John. According to this gospel, the first public
act of Jesus was to transform jars of water into wine—the typical Dionysian epiphany miracle. By employing this well-known Dionysian
convention, the Gospel at its outset establishes the presence of Jesus
as a divine epiphany.[10] To dismiss the Dionysian use of wine simply
as the occasion for mere drunken revelry and debauchery—which did
occur—would be as misleading as to understand the Christian use of
wine similarly—which also occurred, for example, according to Paul,
in the sacramental excesses practiced by the Corinthian church
(I Cor. 11:17–22).

A second emblem common to the diversity of Dionysian communities in the Hellenistic period was the *liknon,* an oblong wicker
basket with handles that was used from ancient times to toss grain
into the wind so the chaff would be blown away.[11] This same basket
was also widely used as a cradle. Pottery and reliefs show the *liknon,*
often covered with a cloth, being carried on the heads of those partici-
pating in Dionysian processions. The *liknon* of Dionysian ritual contained the mask of the god or, what was imagistically equivalent,
vegetation and fruit—often clusters of grapes—from which arose an
erect phallus.

Even as the *liknon* was used to purify grain by tossing it upward
into the wind, so the Dionysian *liknon* represented the possibility of
an ecstatic purification by the breath of the spirit as initiates ritually
transcended the conditions of everydayness.[12] This image of separat-

ing wheat from the chaff through the agency of spirit was also employed by the early Christians (Matt. 3:11–12; Luke 3:16–17).

Grounded in the classical tales of Dionysus's journey to and return from the underworld, and in the parallel stories of his divine rebirth, the Hellenistic Mysteries of Dionysus ensured a happy afterlife. As Plutarch wrote to his wife following the death of their young daughter:

> I know that you are kept from believing the statements of that other sect [the Epicureans] who win many to their way of thinking when they say that nothing is in any way evil or painful to "what has undergone dissolution" [*Ep. Men.* 124] by the teaching of our fathers and by the mystic formulas of the Dionysian rites, the knowledge of which we who are participants share with each other.
>
> *Cons. ad Uxor.* 611, 10

This concern with an afterlife may have been more important in the widespread Egyptian cult of Dionysus, as suggested by his identification with Osiris, the ancient Egyptian deity of the afterlife. However, for the Greeks and Romans the happy Dionysian afterlife was simply the logical extension of a sensuous and happy this-worldly existence that was guaranteed by the wine-drinking festivals and lavish banquets held under the patronage of this deity of life.[13]

The Orgies of the Roman Bacchanalia

The Roman historian Livy (59 B.C.E.–17 C.E.) recorded an investigation into Bacchic excesses reported in Rome, which resulted in a senatorial decree in 186 B.C.E. suppressing the Bacchanalia. His account (in Book 39) is the major literary source for the Dionysian Mysteries in the Hellenistic era.

According to Livy's account, reports about Bacchanalian excesses in Rome came to official attention in connection with the case of Aebutius. Aebutius's mother was more devoted to her second husband, who had squandered his stepson's inheritance, than she was to her son. Consequently, she plotted with her husband to free themselves from Aebutius's unwanted presence by encouraging his initiation into the Bacchanalia, which they were certain would corrupt him. However, Aebutius's mistress, Hispala, warned him about the dangers of this cult, for when she had been a slave, she had accompanied her former mistress to the Bacchic shrine and knew it well as a "factory of all sorts of corruptions." When Aebutius subsequently refused to have anything to do with these Mysteries, his mother and stepfather drove him forcibly from their home. Upon the advice of his aunt, with whom he found refuge, Aebutius presented his case to the consul Spurius Postumius. Postumius summoned Hispala to testify about the rites, which "were usually performed in the nocturnal orgies at the Bacchanalia in the grove of Stimula."

Livy recorded the testimony of Hispala before the consul Postumius on the "origin of the mysteries" as follows:

> At first, she said, it was a ritual for women, and it was the custom that no man should be admitted to it. There had been three days appointed each year on which they held initiations into the Bacchic rites by day; it was the rule to choose the matrons in turn as priestesses. Paculla Annia, a Campanian, she said, when priestess, had changed all this; for she had been the first to initiate men, her sons, Minius and Herennius Cerrinius; she had held the rites by night and not by day, and instead of a mere three days a year she had established five days of initiation in every month. From the time that the rites were performed in common, men mingling with women and the freedom of darkness added, no form of crime, no sort of wrongdoing, was left untried. There were more lustful practices among men with one another than among women. If any of them were disinclined to endure abuse or reluctant to commit crime, they were sacrificed as victims. To consider nothing wrong, she continued, was the highest form of religious devotion among them. Men, as if insane, with fanatical tossings of their bodies, would utter prophecies. Matrons in the dress of Bacchantes, with dishevelled hair and carrying blazing torches, would run down to the Tiber, and plunging their torches in the water (because they contained live sulphur mixed with calcium) would bring them out still burning. Men were alleged to have been carried off by the gods who had been bound to a machine and borne away out of sight to hidden caves: they were those who had refused either to conspire or to join in the crimes or to suffer abuse. Their number, she said, was very great, almost constituting a second state; among them were certain men and women of high rank. Within the last two years it had been ordained that no one beyond the age of twenty years should be initiated: such ages could be involved in error and also were ready to permit abuse.
>
> *Livy* 39, 13, 8–14

Hispala's central charge against the Bacchanalia seems to be: "to consider nothing wrong . . . was the highest form of religious devotion." This moralistically phrased description of the ecstatic core of the Dionysian Mysteries may well have raised the specter of social anarchy familiar from Euripides's popular drama; this description may well locate the ecstatic core of the Dionysian Mysteries. In the view of the Roman Senate, possession by Dionysius was madness and aberration, an anarchistic threat to public order. Because Bacchus had been accepted as a member of the official pantheon, however, his worship could not be forbidden. Nevertheless, following Postumius's presentation of Hispala's testimony to the Senate, it was severely restricted. The practice of the Bacchanalia was forbidden apart from official permission and then was limited to five persons—not more than two men and three women at any celebration—and cult officials and a common treasury were prohibited. This effectively discouraged any organized coherency of the Mysteries with their perceived threat to the state.

According to Livy's report, the rustic deity of drink was most attractive to those on the fringe of society. The vegetation imagery associated with Dionysus, rather than preserving clues to his evolutionary origin, represent the confessional affirmations of rural Greece and southern Italy. The end of the Republic, however, saw a revival of the Bacchic orgies among the upper classes,[14] as is affirmed by Dionysian murals in their homes—for example, in the famous Villa dei Misteri just outside Pompeii.[15]

Orpheus

Orphism, an ancient religio-philosophical tradition, incorporated elements of Dionysian myth in its full-blown cosmology. A Greek hero, Orpheus was considered a historical founder of Orphism and, some would say, a prophet and reformer of the Dionysian Mysteries.[16] He was from Thrace, child of one of the Muses, usually thought to be Calliope, and depending upon the account, of Apollo or of the Thracian river-god Oeagrus.

According to classical references, Orpheus, unlike the typical warrior hero, was a peace-loving patron of the arts, especially of music. Because of a prophecy, Jason included Orpheus among his heroic crew of Argonauts in their search for the golden fleece. The Argonauts were spared seduction by the Siren's song because of Orpheus's own magical singing.[17] When Orpheus's wife, Eurydice, died from a snake bite, the despondent Orpheus descended into the

underworld and charmed Hades and Persephone through the magic
of his song. They released Eurydice on the condition that Orpheus
not turn to look upon her until they had completed their journey from
the underworld. But the anxious Orpheus prematurely turned to ver-
ify his wife's presence, and she vanished forever into the realm of
Hades.[18] Orpheus met his own death, according to one tradition,
when he was dismembered by Thracian women jealous of his devotion to Eurydice. According to Aeschylus's tragedy, *The Bassarae,*
the women were acting on behalf of Dionysus in revenge against
Orpheus for the Olympian flavor of his reforms.[19] In any case, they
threw the head of Orpheus into the Hebrus River, and it floated to
the isle of Lesbos, where, caught upon the rocks, it continued to sing
and deliver oracles.[20]

Parallels between the myth of Orpheus and that of Dionysus are
apparent in these traditions: their common origin in Thrace, their sea
journeys, their wandering that led both to the underworld in quest of
the feminine principle—Dionysus's successful rescue of his mother,
Orpheus's unsuccessful rescue of his wife—the similar death of each
by dismemberment, and their association with oracles. Yet Dionysus
embodied the elemental principle of nature, whereas Orpheus, who
retained a closeness to his father, Apollo, Dionysus's opposite brother, embodied civilization. Thus, the first century B.C.E. historian
Diodorus Siculus wrote:

> Orpheus, the son of Oeagrus, who was the superior of all men in
> natural gifts and education, learned from his father; Orpheus also
> made many changes in the practices and for that reason the rites
> which had been established by Dionysus were also called "Orphic."
> *Diod. Sic.* III, 65, 6

Diodorus also compared Orphic literature with the Eleusinian Mysteries, whose teachings, he claimed, agree with those "which are set
forth in the Orphic poems and are introduced into their rites, but it is
not lawful to recount them in detail to the uninitiated" (*Diod. Sic.* III,
62, 8). Nevertheless, contemporary references to Orphism were to its
literature and life style and not to its cultic practices.

The Orphic Myth of Dionysus

Orphic literature focuses on the overlapping themes of theogony,
cosmogony, and anthropogony. Their unity is summarized in the Or-

phic principle attributed by the early third-century c.e. writer Diogenes Laertes to Museus, the pupil of Orpheus:

All things proceed from unity and are resolved again into unity.

Diog. Laert. Pro. 3

The so-called Rhapsodic Theogony, dated as early as the first century b.c.e.,[21] preserved a composite version of Orphic myth, which was the Hellenistic standard.[22] According to this version,[23] Chronos (Time) in the beginning created the One, represented in the Orphic cosmogony as the silver egg of the cosmos. The bisexual Dionysus-Phanes, known to the Orphics also as Protogonos (First-Born), and as Eros, the creative principle, burst out of this cosmic egg. Phanes, who ruled over the Golden Age, the first Orphic age, created Nyx (Night), and with his daughter, Night, gave birth to Ge and Ouranos (Earth and Heaven). Ge and Ouranos in turn gave birth to the Titans, among others. One of the Titans, Cronos, sealed his supremacy over the other gods by castrating his father, Ouranos. Thus, a first Orphic age was defined by the successive rules of Phanes, Nyx, Ouranos, and Cronos.

Cronos had children by Rhea, but fearing the same treatment from them that he had shown his father, eliminated his offspring by swallowing them. However, their mother, Rhea, was able to save Zeus by substituting a stone that caused Cronos to regurgitate his offspring. Zeus in turn swallowed Phanes, embodying in himself the previous age and thereby securing his rule over a second Orphic age. This second epoch was the present age of mortals and provided the setting for the Orphic anthropogony.

According to Orphic anthropogony, Zeus with his daughter, Persephone, gave birth (or rebirth) to a second Dionysus, Dionysus-Zagreus. His rule over the world as the son of Zeus, as well as over the underworld as the son of Persephone, aroused the envy of the Titans, who, according to some accounts, were also goaded by Hera's jealousy over Zeus's relationship with Persephone. In a Dionysian rage, the Titans dismembered, roasted, and devoured the young Dionysus-Zagreus. But Zeus incinerated the Titans with a thunderbolt, and from their ashes arose the human race. Humans were thus constituted from the evil nature of the Titans, the sons of earth, but also from the divine Dionysus, whom the Titans had eaten. In this way, according to Orphic understanding, the divine Dionysian soul had been imprisoned in the body (in Greek, *soma*) and must be liberated from this prison (in Greek, *sema,* meaning prison or tomb) in order to regain its true nature. One must flee the Titanic in order to save the Dionysian.

The Titans had devoured all but the heart of the young Dionysus-Zagreus, which was recovered by Athena. Zeus swallowed this heart and thereby gave rebirth to Dionysus with Semele. This resurrected Dionysus was able to assist humans in purifying themselves of their Titanic nature and in recalling their true Dionysian self. He thus became one of the Hellenistic saviors.

Orphic writings include a collection of eighty-seven hymns dated from the late Hellenistic period. These hymns, attributed to Orpheus and addressed to different deities, emphasize the cosmic concerns of Orphic literature. The Orphic understanding of human existence expressed in these hymns shared the general Hellenistic view of a problematic existence under the inconstant rule of Tyche/Fortuna expressed in terms of cosmic structures. This cosmic assumption is clear from the Orphic hymn "To Ouranos":

> Ouranos, father of all, eternal cosmic element,
> primeval, beginning of all and end of all,
> lord of the universe, moving about the earth like a sphere,
> home of the blessed gods. Your motion is a roaring whirl,
> and you envelop all as their celestial and terrestrial guard.
> In your breast lies nature's invincible drive.
>
> 4, 1–6[24]

"Nature's invincible drive" refers to the astrologically influenced Hellenistic understanding of fate as is clear from the Orphic hymn "To The Stars":

> Heavenly stars, dear children of dark Night,
> on circles you march and whirl about,
> O brilliant and fiery begetters of all.
> Fate, everyone's fate you reveal,
> and you determine the divine path for mortals
> as, wandering in midair, you gaze upon the seven luminous
>   orbits.
>
> 7, 3–8

The effect of fate upon the Titanic nature of human existence is manifest as the capriciousness of Tyche. In the hymn addressed "To Tyche," we read:

In you lies the great variety of men's livelihood.
To some you grant a wealth of blessings and possessions,
    while to others, against whom you harbor anger, you give evil
        poverty.

72, 6–8

Orphism, then, understood human existence under the rule of Tyche/
Fortuna as fallen, and consequently understood mortal life as a period of punishment and purification.

Orphic Mysteries

The name Orpheus conferred authority upon certain "mysteriosoph-
ical" writings[25] and upon an ascetic life style.[26] Whether there was
any Orphic cult or mystery beyond this is debated. There are indisput-
able examples of local Orphic groups,[27] although recent studies
speak increasingly of an Orphic bearing or attitude that permeated
ancient and Hellenistic thought.[28]

   If it is possible to speak of Orphic Mysteries apart from their
association with the Dionysian cult, they were communicated through
literature and not ritual.[29] The second-century traveller Pausanias
equated the reading of Orphic writings with actually witnessing the
Eleusinian Mysteries (I, 37, 4). Such "literary Mysteries" preserved
the outward form of a Hellenistic mystery religion in the written
word. If the reader of such a literary mystery had turned away from
the world, as evinced by an ascetic life style, this literary presentation
could affect him just as if he had ritually participated in an actual
mystery ritual.[30]

   More striking to Hellenistic observers of Orphism than any sup-
posed ritual practices were their ascetic practices by which they
sought purification from their fortuitous Titanic nature. For it was
through this ascetic purification that the soul, the Dionysian self
within, would be reunited with the One from which it derived and to
which it would ultimately return.

Judaism

As with the Orphics, the life style of the Jews, more than their official
ritual practices celebrated only at the Jerusalem temple, distinguished

them in the Hellenistic world. After Cyrus the Great of Persia liberated the Jews from their Babylonian exile in 536 B.C.E., they were under Persian rule until 332 B.C.E., when Alexander annexed their "Promised Land" into his Macedonian empire following his defeat of the Persian army at Issus the previous year. With the death of Alexander, Palestine came under the rule of the Ptolemies of Egypt until 198 B.C.E., when this rule was usurped by the Seleucids of Syria.

In addition to the Jews who had elected to remain in Babylonia, both Syria and Egypt had attracted large Jewish settlements, and a Jewish community was known in Rome from the mid-second century B.C.E. By the second century, the Greek-speaking Jewish community of Alexandria had produced a Greek translation of the Hebrew Scriptures known as the Septuagint, "the Seventy," after a tradition of seventy-two inspired translators.[31]

The diaspora communities of Jews generally prospered under official policies of religious toleration. However, in 167 B.C.E. Antiochus IV of Syria reversed this policy and attempted to transform Jerusalem into a Greek city, a plan that included the suppression of Jewish practices and the dedication of the Temple of Yahweh to Olympian Zeus. This open attempt at Hellenization brought about a successful revolt of the Jews led by the priest Judas Maccabaeus, the Jewish rededication of their temple to Yahweh in 164, and a more or less independent Jewish state for the next one hundred years. In 63 B.C.E. the Roman general Pompey intervened in an internal dispute over the succession of rule and thereby established the precedent for a formal annexation by Rome of Judea, Samaria, and Idumaea in 6 C.E. as the province of Judea.

A tradition of normative Judaism, which endured foreign domination and successfully resisted Hellenization under Ptolemaic and Seleucid rule, has often been assumed, at least for Palestine. Although the purity of Yahweh worship was unquestionably a concern of Judaism during the Hellenistic period as throughout its history, it was maintained largely as a theological ideal rather than as historical reality. Many Jews enthusiastically elected to live the cosmopolitan life of the Hellenistic world. The second-century B.C.E. apocryphal book of I Maccabees even reported that some Palestinian Jews, in order to participate in the Greek games, submitted to "uncircumcision" (I Macc. 1:10–15), a legal and literal repudiation of their covenant with Yahweh and thus of their Jewish identity. Although such acts undoubtedly represent an uncharacteristic extreme of Hellenistic Judaism and are cited by I Maccabees as part of the reason for the Maccabean revolt, they nevertheless call into question the assumption of a Judaism significantly untainted by Hellenism.

A conflict between the Jewish covenantal ideal of pure Yahweh worship and the impinging influences of non-Jewish culture and cult had informed the history of the Jews from their beginnings. According to the book of Exodus, when Moses descended Mt. Sinai with the tablets of the covenant, he found that his followers "had turned aside quickly from the way which the Lord had commanded" by fashioning for themselves a "molten calf," an image of deity favored in Canaan (Exod. 32:1–6). Subsequent seductive and pervasive non-Jewish practices provided the *raison d'être* for the prophetic tradition of Israel, which devoted itself to the ideal of an untainted, pure Yahweh worship.

Hellenistic Judaism

The writings of the first century C.E. Jewish historian Flavius Josephus (circa 37–95 C.E.), and of his contemporary, the Jewish philosopher Philo Judaeus (circa 30 B.C.E.–45 C.E.), exemplify the relation of Palestinian and diaspora Judaism to their cultural and historical context in the Hellenistic period.

An aristocrat among the Jews, Josephus was characteristically an advocate of Hellenistic culture, yet he was also a vigorous defender of Judaism. When he failed to persuade his countrymen of the futility of rebellion against the might of Rome in 66 C.E., he accepted the military command of Galilee. In 67 he was captured by Vespasian's troops, but because he predicted that Vespasian would become emperor, his life was spared and he was imprisoned. When his captor indeed was acclaimed emperor in 69, Josephus was released. Following the fall of Jerusalem in 70, he settled in Rome, where he produced, under imperial patronage, major works on Judaism for his Roman audience: *The Jewish War,* written from 75 to 79, and *Jewish Antiquities,* written from 93 to 94.

Philo Judaeus, in contrast, was a leader of the large Jewish community in Alexandria, the intellectual and cultural center of the Roman Empire. Like Josephus, he was an apologist for Judaism to the Greco-Roman world. Yet unlike Josephus, who was a Jew attracted to the Hellenistic culture of Rome, Philo was a thoroughly Hellenized citizen of cosmopolitan Alexandria who was also a Jew. He was a Platonist who argued that everything good, true, and beautiful among the Greeks in actuality had been derived by Plato from Moses. To the extent that he was representative, this Jewish thinker is the primary source for Hellenistic Jewish thought outside Palestine.

Reflecting upon Jewish alternatives in the Hellenistic period, Josephus wrote:

> Now at this time there were three schools of thought among the Jews, which held different opinions concerning human affairs; the first being that of the Pharisees, the second that of the Sadducees, and the third that of the Essenes. *AJ* XIII, 171

The Sadducees were an openly pro-Hellenistic movement whose Judaism consisted of strict Yahweh worship in the temple services but who otherwise participated fully in the life of their contemporary world. They accepted as binding only the written Mosaic law, rejecting the oral tradition of interpretation and consequently many of the practices and customs that had come to characterize Judaism as a separatist life style. Their rejection of the binding nature of oral tradition undoubtedly reflected something of Hellenistic individualism.

The Pharisees, however, championed not only the binding nature of the written law but also the authority of the orally transmitted traditions of the elders who had adapted the written law to changing historical conditions. Adherence to the practices and customs that had developed from this tradition resulted in an anti-Hellenistic, separatist stance.

Philo similarly described these two trends within contemporary Judaism:

> There are some who, regarding laws in their literal sense in the light of symbols of matters belonging to the intellect, are overpunctilious about the latter, while treating the former with easy-going neglect. Such men I for my part should blame for handling the matter in too easy and off-hand a manner: they ought to have given careful attention to both aims, to a more full and exact investigation of what is not seen and in what is seen to be stewards without reproach. As it is, as though they were living alone by themselves in a wilderness, or as though they had become disembodied souls, and know neither city nor village nor household nor any company of human beings at all, overlooking all that the mass of men regard, they explore reality in all its naked absoluteness. These men are taught by the sacred word to have thought for good repute, and to let go nothing that is part of the customs fixed by divinely empowered men greater than those of our time. *Mig.* 89–90

The Sadducees were those who accepted only "what is seen," that is, the literal interpretation of written law; the Pharisees were those who accepted, in addition, "what is not seen," that is, the oral law with its traditional and allegorical interpretations.

Josephus described a third party, the Essenes, whose beliefs resembled those of the Pharisees but who carried separatism further by retreating to isolated settlements where they sought to maintain ceremonial purity through ascetic practice. However, the discovery in 1947 of the Dead Sea Scrolls, an Essene library from Qumran, showed the effect of Hellenistic influence upon the life and thought of even this separatist movement. *The Manual of Discipline* from this library, for example, teaches a knowledge reserved only for initiates and which was structured in terms of a cosmic dualism. (Philo writes also of the Therapeutae, a Jewish group who lived in the Alexandrian desert a life even more cloistered than that of the Essenes (*Cont.*).)

Finally, Josephus identified a group that he characterized as agreeing "in all other respects with the opinions of the Pharisees, except that they have a passion for liberty that is almost unconquerable, since they are convinced that God alone is their leader and master" (*AJ* XVIII, 23). Although unnamed by Josephus, this party is generally identified with the Zealots, an anti-Roman, revolutionary group.

Josephus differentiated the three major Jewish philosophies on the basis of their relationship to fate (in Greek, *heimarmenē*):

> As for the Pharisees, they say that certain events are the work of Fate [*heimarmenē*], but not all; as to other events, it depends upon ourselves whether they shall take place or not. The sect of Essenes, however, declares that Fate is mistress of all things, and that nothing befalls men unless it be in accordance with her decree. But the Sadducees do away with Fate, holding that there is no such thing and that human actions are not achieved in accordance with her decree, but that all things lie within our own power, so that we ourselves are responsible for our well-being, while we suffer misfortune through our own thoughtlessness.   *AJ* XIII, 172–173

To a first-century reader, *heimarmenē* most probably carried the astrological significance of the deterministic powers of the material cosmos. Originally a Stoic concept that expressed the philosophical assumption of natural order, *heimarmenē* was reappropriated in popular thought to name the negative aspects of that order.[32] According to the Qumran scrolls, the Essenes agree that this world was ruled by such powers of darkness. Similarly, Paul, writing to a Jewish-Christian audience in Galatia, characterized Jewish practice as enslavement to the "elemental spirits of the universe" (Gal. 4:3–10), a phrase equivalent to the astrological meaning of *heimarmenē*. It is striking that Paul, a Jewish contemporary of Josephus, used the same criterion to characterize Judaism as a whole which Josephus used to differentiate schools within Judaism. Because there is no Hebrew equivalent for the important Greek concept of *heimarmenē,* Josephus's characterization of contemporary Judaism in terms of this cosmic structure of existence establishes a Jewish self-understanding in terms of its Hellenistic cultural context.[33]

Josephus characterized the Pharisees as attributing everything to *heimarmenē* as well as to God (*BJ* II, 8, 14). Thus Josephus, who was most likely a Pharisee, understood human existence in terms both of *heimarmenē,* the natural order of the Hellenistic world in which he found himself, and of Torah, the requirements of God and his rule mediated through Mosaic law. Josephus thereby accommodated the Hellenistic feminine natural order of things to Torah, the divine law of Yahweh, creator and ruler of the cosmos, who represented a masculine alternative to the feminine order. By contrast, Philo challenged the finality of *heimarmenē* and concluded that God was, in fact, the sole ruler of the cosmos (*Mig.* 179; *Quis rer. div.* 300–301).

Neither the cosmic assumption that characterized the Hellenistic world nor the feminine attributes inherent in this cosmic stance were alien to Judaism. Incursions of the feminine into the patriarchal nature of Yahweh worship dated from the conflict between this god and the chthonic Baals of Canaan. Once again, as Judaism entered the Hellenistic world its patriarchal tradition was challenged by the feminine principle.

Yahweh and the Feminine

The emergence of a strong feminine element into the patriarchal formulations of traditional Judaism is indicated by one of two related religious types for which Hellenistic Judaism is exemplary: apocalyptic and wisdom.[34] Both assume the cosmic or vertical imagery afforded by Ptolemaic cosmology for structuring Judaism's revelatory message. In apocalyptic myth (from the Greek, *apokalypsis,* meaning "revelation" or "disclosure"), a prophet or seer typically embarks on

a journey through the heavens during which divine secrets concerning
an immanent end time are disclosed.[35] Similarly in wisdom myth, a
prophet or seer may ascend to the presence of a divine Wisdom of
God which is hid away in heaven (see, for instance, Job 28); or a
personified Wisdom of God herself may descend into the midst of
human history (see, for example, Proverbs 8).

The ancient image of the Wisdom of Yahweh (see, for instance,
Deut. 4:6) came to express for Hellenistic Judaism a feminine principle that ordered the cosmos:

> She [Wisdom] reaches mightily from one end of the earth to the
> other, and she orders all things well.   Wisd. of Sol. 8:1

By the late third century B.C.E., Wisdom (in Greek, *Sophia*) appeared
as a personified cosmological consort of Yahweh (Prov. 3:19). Thus
for Philo, Moses, the source of Jewish wisdom as well as of Greek
knowledge, was

> the child of parents incorruptible and wholly free from stain, his
> father being God, who is likewise Father of all, and his mother Wis-
> dom, through whom the universe came into existence.
>
> *Fug.* 109

The personification of this Hellenistic cosmic and feminine counterpart to, or consort of, Yahweh generally drew upon the characteristic traits of the Hellenistic goddesses and especially upon the imagery
of the wisest of the goddesses, Isis. Even as the Hellenistic goddess of
the cosmos opposed and was opposed by chaotic Tyche/Fortuna, so
the Jewish Sophia, the cosmic principle of order, was opposed by the
figure of "the foolish woman" or Folly, the cosmic principle of disorder. This antithetical structure is recounted in the biblical book of
Proverbs in which the two sisters, Folly and Wisdom, call out to man:

> With much seductive speech she [Folly] persuades him [a young
> man of the world]; with her smooth talk she compels him. All at
> once he follows her, as an ox goes to the slaughter, or as a stag is
> caught fast till an arrow pierces its entrails; as a bird rushes into a
> snare; he does not know that it will cost him his life.
>
> Prov. 7:21–23

Does not wisdom call, does not understanding raise her voice? On the heights beside the way, in the paths she takes her stand; beside the gates in front of the town, at the entrance of the portals she cries aloud.   Prov. 8:1–3

The call of Folly is a seduction into death (Prov. 7: 10–27). The call of Wisdom, however, leads to life and salvation (Prov. 2–3).

Wisdom and Folly, like Isis and Demeter, both wander through the cosmos. But Folly "is loud and wayward, her feet do not stay at home" (Prov. 7:11). Wisdom, on the other hand,

came forth from the mouth of the Most High, and covered the earth like a mist. I [Wisdom] dwelt in high places, and my throne was in a pillar of cloud. Alone I have made the circuit of the vault of heaven and have walked in the depths of the abyss. In the waves of the sea, in the whole earth, and in every people and nation I have gotten a possession. Among all these I sought a resting place; I sought in whose territory I might lodge.   Sirach 24:3–7

As Isis found her home among the Egyptians, so Wisdom came to her home among the Jews;

Then the Creator of all things gave me [Wisdom] a commandment, and the one who created me assigned a place for my tent. And he said, "Make your dwelling in Jacob, and in Israel receive your inheritance."   Sirach 24:8

And just as Isis might lead one to Osiris, so Wisdom leads one to Yahweh:

The beginning of wisdom is the most sincere desire for instruction, and concern for instruction is love of her, and love of her is the keeping of her laws, and giving heed to her laws is assurance of immortality, and immortality brings one near to God; so the desire for wisdom leads to a kingdom.   Wisd. of Sol. 6:17–20

Although the Jewish figure of personified Wisdom was modeled upon the Hellenistic goddesses, her myth never became ritualized as part of Jewish practice. Yet there is some evidence that mystery practices left their mark upon some Jewish communities. Philo, for example, referred to the Judaism into which he had been "initiated under Moses" as a mystery (*Cher.* 48).[36] Further, he described the Therapeutae by analogy to the Mysteries:

> In each house there is a consecrated room which is called a sanctuary or closet and closeted in this they are initiated into the mysteries of the sanctified life.   *Cont.* 25

Also, he employed Dionysian imagery to describe a portion of their collective rites:

> Then when each choir has separately done its own part in the feast, having drunk as in the Bacchic rites of the strong wine of God's love they mix and both together become a single choir.   *Cont.* 85

Whether the Therapeutae actually had adopted Dionysian imagery and practices or whether Philo employed this imagery to communicate something of this Jewish group to his Hellenistic audience, it is clear that the worship of Yahweh and that of Dionysus were comparable for some in the Hellenistic world. The striking appearance of Dionysian-Orphic symbols in the third-century C.E. wall paintings of the Dura-Europas synagogue in eastern Syria confirms that Philo's references to Bacchic symbols and images in a Jewish context were not anomalies of some Egyptian-Jewish fringe group or reflections of his own interpretation.[37] Indeed, the Jewish god was identified by some with Sabazios, an ancient Thraco-Phrygian deity who most often was identified with Dionysus.[38] This identification was justified by the questionable etymological similarities between Lord "Sabazios" and the biblical attribution of Yahweh as Lord "Sebaoth," the Lord of Hosts.

With the fall of Jerusalem and the destruction of the temple by the Roman legions in 70 C.E. and with the failure of a final Jewish revolt in 135 C.E., priestly and Sadducean Judaism disappeared from the historical arena. The Zealots were largely destroyed in their resistance to the superior military power of Rome. Judaism as a cultic and political entity no longer existed; only the law and its rich oral tradition remained the unchallenged basis of Jewish identity— and Jewish law with its strict theological ideal of pure Yahweh worship admitted no place for the Hellenistic feminine principle. Consequently, Judaism emerged in the late Hellenistic world as the rabbinic Judaism of the synagogue with its teaching and worship of the patriarchal Yahweh.

The movement from an early Hellenistic sovereignty of the feminine to a late Hellenistic masculine structure was not limited to the challenge of rabbinic Judaism to the influence of the cosmic goddess of the Mysteries but was representative of a structural shift throughout the Hellenistic world. Masculine patterns of redemption came to be the common reality underlying and allowing for the religious patterns of late antiquity.

INNOVATIONS

Alexander of Abonoteichus

The most striking example of a newly created cult in the Hellenistic period is the oracle and Mysteries of Glycon, invented during the second century c.e. by Alexander of Abonoteichus. The origin of this cult is documented by a contemporary of Alexander, Lucian of Samasota, in his treatise on *Alexander the False Prophet*. Although this satirical exposé of Alexander's cult must be contrasted with the propagandistic witness of an Apuleius, for example, or with the Christian writings of the New Testament, Lucian's account is corroborated by gems, coins, and inscriptions.[39]

Alexander began his career in the service of a certain physician who, in Lucian's estimate, was a quack. This physician was a follower of Apollonius of Tyana, an itinerate sage, who had traveled widely throughout Asia Minor, Persia, India, Egypt, and Rome, proclaiming his message of ascetic purity, healing the sick, exorcising demons, and attempting a reform of pagan cultic practices. As with his contemporary, Jesus, with whom he was later compared,[40] signs and miracles were said to have accompanied Apollonius's birth, and some said that upon his death, he ascended bodily into heaven. Although his reputation was defended by Philostratus, the second-century c.e. sophist who wrote a *Life of Apollonius* based upon the memoirs of Apollonius's companion Damis, Lucian considered him to be a charlatan along with Alexander.[41]

Following the death of his physician patron, Alexander formed a partnership with a certain Cocconas, and the two "went about the country practising quackery and sorcery, and 'trimming the fatheads'—for so they style the public in the traditional patter of magicians" (*Alex.* 6). After lining their pockets at the expense of a "rich Macedonian woman, past her prime but still eager to be charming," they devised a plan to expand their activities by founding a prophetic shrine and oracle. The aspiring holy men planted some bronze tablets in the ancient Apollo temple at Chalcedon, which prophesized that Asclepius would soon appear at Abonoteichus, a small town in northern Asia Minor. When these tablets were "discovered," word quickly reached the divinely ordained town, and its citizenry immediately began to prepare for the deity's advent by excavating for a new temple. Shortly, Alexander himself arrived in Abonoteichus, outfitted in the robes of a prophet, wearing long hair, and effecting fits of ecstatic madness by chewing the root of soapwort so that his mouth would foam. Meanwhile, Cocconas had died in Chalcedon, so it was now left to Alexander to reinforce the oracles of the bronze tablets with his own person, prophecies, and even claim of divine descent.

"When it was time to begin," Alexander came one day into the marketplace effecting the frenzy of "a devotee of the Great Mother," and spoke exotic-sounding gibberish to an excited crowd that had gathered around his theatrical performance. Then he ran to the site of the new temple, drawing the crowd with him. Singing hymns in honor of Asclepius and Apollo, he retrieved from the muddy excavations a blown goose-egg containing a baby snake, which he had hidden there the evening before. He then broke open the egg and revealed to the amazed crowd the "twice-born Asclepius" contained therein.

Several days later, after popular anticipation had spread, Alexander announced that the new deity was ready to receive devotees. Sitting upon a couch in a dim room, Alexander had coiled a large serpent around his body, its head hidden under his arm and by his full beard. In place of the serpent's concealed head, he displayed a dummy humanoid head realistically constructed of linen, and whose mouth and tongue he could manipulate with horsehair controls. The impressionable crowds were astonished that the tiny Asclepius of a few days earlier had so rapidly matured into so great and distinctive a deity.

Glycon, the grandson of Zeus, as Alexander styled this new Asclepius, was now ready to deliver prophecies. At first, the oracle answered questions that were submitted upon a sealed scroll. The "unopened" scroll was later returned containing a reply from the god, composed, of course, by Alexander or one of his paid oracle writers. Luciun details several methods of undoing sealed scrolls in such a way that they appear to be unopened (*Alex.* 21). Later, the oracle prophesied directly, and more dramatically, by means of a speaking tube constructed from cranes' windpipes and manned by one of Alexander's confederates. Finally, Alexander even established a "celebration of mysteries" modeled upon the Eleusinian, complete with torchlight ceremonies and a priesthood (*Alex.* 38–43). Participation in these mysteries ensured "good fortune" (*agathē tychē*) for its participants (*Alex.* 42). By combining the nostalgic appeal of oracular piety with the popular appeal of mystery practices, and by charging substantially for each oracle spoken, Alexander did indeed prosper.

The fame of this incarnate deity of Abonoteichus and of his prophet, Alexander, spread through "the whole Roman Empire," a fame enhanced when Alexander dispatched many of his deputies abroad to report on the oracle's fantastic predictions, on the healings, and even on the resurrections from the dead that they claimed had occurred at the oracle. In addition, he secured the patronage of Rutilanus, a Roman nobleman and official who married Alexander's daughter, Selene, at the urging of the divine oracle.

Although Alexander's cult survived him (he died about 170) by a hundred years, two new religions of the period met with considerably more success. In contrast to Alexander's claim of a new Mystery of Abonoteichus, both Mithraism, founded during the first century B.C.E., and Christianity attempted to disguise their novelty by claiming ancient origins. This criterion of ancient origins was claimed also for the other Mysteries—for example, those of Isis—and by the philosophical traditions in their appeal to Pythagoras or Plato. Mithraism's claim to ancient Persian beginnings was so successful that it was not seriously challenged until the 1970s. Christianity's claim to be the true heir of Abraham and of ancient Israel (for instance, Paul in Gal. 3) was compromised, however, by Rome's official if grudging acceptance of Judaism's antiquity, by Judaism's rejection of Christianity, and by Christianity's own claim to a new revelation.

Mithraism

The Origin of Mithraism

Mithraism has been treated as a Hellenistic mystery by its contemporary and modern interpreters alike. Like the cults imported from the East, Mithraism was an initiatory cult concerned with overcoming the vicissitudes of an apparently chaotic world. Yet Mithraism exhibited none of the chthonic character of the other Mysteries. It was a cult in honor of the Great God Mithras to which only males were admitted.

The odyssey of Mithras began among the ancient Indo-Aryan peoples. He traveled east to India, where the Vedic literature associated Mithras with the supreme deity Varuna, and west to Persia, where the sacred Avestas associated him with the high god Ahura-Mazda. In both India and Persia, Mithras was an agent of the supreme ordainer of the cosmos and ally of the forces that preserve order. In both cultural incarnations this god of light dispelled darkness and upheld righteousness. In the arena of history, Mithras was the protector of kings and the comrade of the enforcers of political order, the armies of empire. Not surprisingly, it was said that Alexander the Great had been initiated into Persian Mithraism, together with many of his subordinates (Pliny, *HN* X, 37; *Pseudo-Callisthenes* III, 34). A Syrian fresco depicts Antiochus I, one of the four heirs to Alexander's empire, shaking hands with Mithras,[42] while the line of succession in Pontus adopted for itself the name Mithradates. The Roman cult of Mithras claimed this ancestry, and a Persian origin for Roman Mithraism remains the prominent interpretation.[43]

Mithraic remains, however, are notably absent from Greek soil, and the evidence of Western Mithraism, documented only since the first century B.C.E. is notably discontinuous from the Persian evidence. Clearly the Roman Mithras must be considered only a distant relative of the Persian deity, perhaps related by name alone. His Western cult, consequently, must have originated somewhere in the Roman East—Plutarch says among the Cilician pirates (*Vit. Pomp.* 24)—or even in the Roman West, given the density of Mithraic remains in this part of the world. The cult swept the Roman world during the first three centuries C.E. until its disappearance following the decrees of Theodosius.

The Myth of Mithras

The few texts describing Mithraism are mostly late and written by its critics. The third-century C.E. philosopher Porphyry knew a multivolumed *History of Mithraism* by the historian Euboulos, which unfortunately has not survived. Knowledge of Western Mithraism must therefore be reconstructed almost entirely from archaeological and iconographic evidence.

Unlike the myths of other mystery deities, no received myth of

Mithras survives, nor does the iconographic evidence seem to reflect any such official narrative of the deity's life. Mithraic iconography seems rather to depict isolated scenes of Mithraic activity from which modern attempts to reconstruct a mythic narrative have been made. Even these scenes, with several exceptions, seem to represent regional variations of cult expression.

A first group of scenes represent Mithras as emerging or being born from a rock, naked except for his characteristically pointed Phrygian cap. He clothes himself with leaves from a nearby fig tree and nourishes himself with its fruit. Depending upon the representation, he is equipped with a dagger as a warrior, with a bow and arrow as a hunter, with a torch as the bringer of light, or with a globe as the ruler of the cosmos. This miraculous birth is witnessed either by shepherds who worship him or by Cautes and Cautopates, two torchbearers common in Mithraic iconography. Other scenes show Mithras breaking open a rock from which water gushes into the cupped hands of a waiting man. Another group of scenes depict him as a hunter.

The only scene common to all Mithraic finds is the famous tauroctony or bull-slaying scene, which has been found on the main or rear wall of virtually every Mithraeum, the Mithraic sanctuary. This icon, a fresco or relief carved from stone, depicts Mithras pinning a fallen bull with his left knee. With his face averted to his right, he pulls the animal's head back by its mouth, chin, or horns with his left hand so that its throat is exposed; with his right hand, he slays the beast with his knife or sword. A sheaf of grain sprouts from the bull's tail. A raven appears over Mithras's right shoulder, often perched on his cloak. A serpent and often a cup are ranged beneath the bull, while a dog laps at the fatal wound of the bull and a scorpion is attached to the dying animal's genitals.

The icon is almost always flanked by the two torchbearers: Cautes, carrying an upright torch, and Cautopates, carrying an inverted torch. It often includes images of the sun and the moon in its upper corners and is sometimes encircled by the signs of the zodiac.

The astral imagery in this icon clearly suggests an astronomical/ astrological significance for the entire icon. The tauroctony in fact represents a map of the heavens centering upon the constellation of Taurus (the bull) and the adjacent constellations of Canis Minor or Major (the dog), Hydra (the serpent), Crater (the cup), Corvus (the raven), and Scorpio (the scorpion), that zodiacal sign which was understood to govern the genitals. The ear of wheat sprouting from the bull's tail may correspond to the star Spica, which is said to represent the ear of grain held by the virgin in the constellation Virgo.[44] Two theories have been proposed to explain why only these constellations and no others appear in the tauroctony. The first theory understands these constellations as those which are visible at a particular time of year;[45] the second holds that they are the constellations that lie on or below the celestial equator with respect to Taurus.[46]

A growing consensus that the figures of the tauroctonous icon correspond in some way to constellations has not, however, resulted in any agreement on the central question concerning the identification of Mithras himself. He has been identified most often with the sun because of his traditional Persian character as a solar deity and because of Latin inscriptions identifying him with *Sol Invictus,* the Invincible Sun. But since the other figures of the tauroctony correspond to constellations, Mithras has been identified with the constellation Orion[47] or (more interestingly, given its position in the heavens directly above Taurus) with the constellation Perseus.[48] Cautes and Cautopates seem to signify antitheses of some sort—such as light/ dark, rising/setting sun, summer/winter, this or that star—depending upon the identification of Mithras. Nor does this concensus on the astronomical significance of the central icon of Mithraism answer the question of its meaning for the cult, although it clearly depicts in some sense an act of salvation.[49] An inscription from the Santa Prisca Mithraeum in Rome, one of the few Mithraic inscriptions to survive from the antiquity states: "Us too you have saved by shedding blood which grants eternity."[50]

The astral or cosmic understanding of the central Mithraic icon is reinforced by the Mithraeum itself, which was structured as an image of the cosmos. The usually small sanctuaries of the Mithraic cult were either caves (natural or carved into solid rock) or structures that simulated caves. Porphyry, citing Euboulos, writes that the

> cave bore . . . the image of the Cosmos which Mithras had created and the things which the cave contained, by their proportionate arrangement, provided him with symbols of the elements and climates of the Cosmos.   *De Antr. Nymph.* 6[51]

The Mithraeum itself, in other words, imaged in some sense the cosmos.[52]

There is a clear contrast between the Mithraic portrayal of the cosmos as sacred in its totality and the Delphic or Eleusinian portrayal of the cosmos as sacred only in relation to their localized precinct. Rather than an adaptation of pre-Hellenistic local pietistic and mystery topographies to the new cosmic structures of the Hellenistic world, Mithraism exemplifies a new cult defined out of and wholly in terms of Hellenistic cosmic structures.

Mithraic Initiation

It was within the Mithraic cave, according to Porphyry, that initiates were introduced to the Mysteries. According to the Christian biblical scholar and apologist Jerome (circa 342–420) and confirmed by archaeological evidence, especially from the Mithraeum of Felicissimus at the Roman port of Ostia, there were seven grades of initiation in the Mithraic Mysteries (Jerome, *Ep.* 107).[53] The first three grades were known as Raven, Nymph or Embryo,[54] and Soldier. The raven as messenger of the gods may represent the invitational or initial grade of instruction. Following such instruction, the *mystae* could then be initiated as Nymph, one in initial or embryonic union with the deity. In the next grade, an initiate might progress to the active stance of a soldier in support of and in full service to his god. As one inscription discovered in the Santa Prisca Mithraeum reads: "And I bore the instructions of the gods on my shoulders to sustain till the end."[55] These three grades seem to have been preparatory, and its members may have been excluded from full participation in the cultic meal.

The cult meal or banquet is the most widely documented Mithraic scene apart from the tauroctony. Sometimes found on a reversible relief of the tauroctony, it depicts Mithras sharing a meal with Sol, the personification of the sun, on the skin of the slain bull. This meal undoubtedly had a central place in the Mithraic cult.

The subsequent four grades of initiation were those of Lion, Perses, Runner of the Sun, and Father. The Lion was the midpoint in the grades of initiation and was associated with fire imagery. Perses, recalling the cult's claim to ancient Persian origins, and Runner of the Sun, recalling Mithras's solar ally, were the next grades of initiation, which culminated in the highest grade, Father.

Although the significance assigned to Mithraic initiation remains largely speculative, according to Celsus, a second-century opponent of Christianity cited by the third-century Christian father Origen (*C. Celsum* VI, 22), it consisted of an ascent through the seven planetary spheres imaged as a ladder with seven rungs. This vertical imagery of initiatory grades suggests a link between heaven and earth parallel to the astronomical imagery of the tauroctony and the cosmic representation of the Mithraeum itself, which completes and offers its initiates a representation of systemic cosmic integration.[57]

The Mithraic structure of redemption may be illustrated by a relatively late (early fourth-century) Greek magical papyrus (Papyrus 574 of the Bibliothèque Nationale, Paris [PGM]). As part of the text purports to contain the revelation of Mysteries by Mithras (PGM 475–834), it has been identified as a Mithras liturgy, by which title these lines are usually known.[58]

The "Mithras Liturgy" opens with the supplication "Be gracious to me, O Providence and Tyche." Later in the text, as the initiate has ascended and beholds the universe, seven virgins appear who are called "the Fates [Tychai] of heaven," and who are hailed as noble, good, and sacred. The locus of this text in a magical papyrus and the inclusion of magical formulae in its contents confirm the late Hellenistic world as the world of magic depicted by Apuleius. But the difference between this world and that of Apuleius is that the world of the magical papyrus is a world to be transcended. It ensures "that I [the initiate] alone may ascend into heaven as an inquirer and behold the universe" (PGM 434–435). It is from this transcendent perspective of the ascended initiate that the seven Tychai are revealed as noble, good, and sacred, for from within the cosmos they could represent only the chaos of chance.

The names of the Mithraic initiatory grades all have in common the systematic exclusion or suppression of the feminine.[59] Mithraism apparently complemented the hierarchic and disciplined structures and values of its male members, primarily drawn from the lower ranks of the military and from among the petty bureaucracy of slaves and freedmen, with a new integrated view of the cosmos now completely structured in terms of masculine attributes and in support of Roman imperial rule.[60]

Christianity

One of the first issues to be debated by Christians was whether they were a new religion. The first followers of Jesus were centered in and around Jerusalem under the leadership of Jesus's brother, James, and two of his disciples, Peter and John. These early Jewish-Christians understood Christianity in terms of its Jewish past and they continued their observance of Jewish ritual practices exemplified by dietary requirements and circumcision.

Paul, in contrast, was concerned with interpreting Christianity to the wider non-Jewish world and argued that Christianity required only an affirmation of faith in Christ. Consequently, in Paul's understanding the requirements of Jewish law were not a necessary prerequisite of the faith. Paul's Christianity had its historical roots in Judaism, but theologically it was an autonomous and thus new religion.

A compromise between Jewish and Pauline gentile Christianity was reached at the Apostolic Council of about 48 C.E. The Jerusalem church would minister to the circumcised, and Paul would minister to "the uncircumcised," that is, to the gentile world (Gal. 2:7–9).

The letters of Paul, dating from about 51 with his First Epistle to the Thessalonians, are the earliest literary sources of Christianity. The later gospels, which recount the life and teachings of Jesus, range from some fifteen to twenty years later with the Gospel of Mark (about 65–70 C.E.) to the end of the first century for the Gospels of Matthew, Luke, and John. Because Paul was the earliest literary witness for Christianity and the interpreter of this new religion to the broader concerns of the Hellenistic world, his understanding of "Jesus as the Christ" provides the clearest example of its relation to that world.

Although Paul was highly educated in the Jewish tradition (Gal. 1:14), he must have been influenced to some extent by the range of religious alternatives present in his native city of Tarsus (according to Acts 21:39; 22:3). Located in Cilicia, one of the suggested regions of origin for Mithraism, Tarsus was a cosmopolitan center important as a crossroads of travel between Syria and Asia Minor to the west, and beyond to Greece and Rome.[61]

Like Paul, Christianity itself emerged from the linguistic and imagistic conventions of the Hellenistic world and belonged to its array of religious alternatives. It was an initiatory cult open to all races, Jewish and Greek; to all classes, slave and free; and, unlike Mithraism, to both male and female (Gal. 3:28). It seemed to adopt a kind of mystery structure by actively and publically proclaiming its message to the unconverted, from whom, however, its full "mystery" remained veiled. As Paul expressed this dichotomy between public sermon and initiate mystery:

> We preach Christ crucified, a stumbling block to Jews and folly to
> Gentiles, but to those who are called, both Jews and Greeks, Christ
> the power of God and the wisdom of God.   I Cor. 1:23–25

Like the Mysteries, Christianity early established a formal initiatory
distinction between the preparatory grade of catechumen, and a par-
ticipatory grade of full communicant.[62]

The Christ Myth

Paul's understanding of Christian existence was not based upon the
historical life and teachings of Jesus, about which his writings show
little knowledge, but upon his claim to a "revelation of Jesus Christ"
(Gal. 1:11–12). The fundamental structure of this "revelation" is
preserved in a so-called Christ-hymn, apparently an early Christian
formulation, cited by Paul in his Epistle to the Philippians:

> [Jesus is the Christ] who, though he was in the form of God,
> did not count equality with God a thing to be grasped,
> but emptied himself,
> taking the form of a servant,
> being born in the likeness of men.
> And being found in human form
> he humbled himself
> and became obedient unto death,
> even death on a cross.
>
> Therefore God has highly exalted him
> and bestowed on him the name
> which is above every name,
> that at the name of Jesus every knee should bow
> in heaven and on earth and under the earth,
> and every tongue confess
> that Jesus Christ is Lord,
> to the glory of God the Father.
>   Phil. 2:6–11

A similar hymnic or creedal passage is found in Colossians:

> [Christ Jesus] is the image of the invisible God,
> the first born of all creation;
> for in him all things were created,

in heaven and on earth, visible and invisible,
whether thrones or dominions or principalities or authorities.

All things were created through him and for him.
He is before all things,
and in him all things hold together.
He is the head of the body, the church;
he is the beginning, the first-born from the dead,
that in everything he might be pre-eminent.
For in him all the fulness of God was pleased to dwell,
and through him to reconcile to himself all things,
whether on earth or in heaven,
making peace by the blood of his cross.

Col. 1:15–20

Both of these passages share basic elements of a cosmic myth: a redeemer who exists before creation, who rules over creation and all the cosmos, who descends ("emptied" and "humbled") from his transcendent origin into the conditions of this world (incarnation, suffering, and death) and re-ascends to his transcendent origin and cosmic rule (resurrection). The structure of this cosmic myth of redemption is maintained in the biographical elaborations of the later gospels: the descent/incarnation motif appears in the images of the baptismal descent of the spirit (Mark 1:10–11), of virgin birth (Matthew and Luke), and in the theological motif of "word [*Logos*] becoming flesh" in the Prologue to the Gospel of John. The ascent motif is preserved throughout Christian tradition in the image of resurrection.[63]

Pauline Christianity assumed the Ptolemaic cosmological structure, as Paul clearly indicates in an autobiographical anecdote:

I know a man in Christ who fourteen years ago was caught up to the third heaven—whether in the body or out of the body I do not know, God knows. And I know that this man was caught up into Paradise—whether in the body or out of the body I do not know, God knows—and he heard things that cannot be told, which man may not utter. II Cor. 12:2–4

The third heaven represented for Paul, as for Judaic apocalyptic thought generally, the place of Paradise (see, for instance, II Enoch 8:1), in which the first heaven represents the celestial realm of the planets collectively and the second heaven refers to the sphere of the fixed stars. The threefold regional differentiation of heaven could be expanded to a planetary seven, as in the case of Jewish *merkabah* mysticism,[64] the Testament of Levi (2 and 3), and the Ascension of Isaiah (6–11).

As a follower of the resurrected/ascendant Christ into the heavenly realm, Paul possesses "the wisdom of God in a mystery, even the hidden wisdom which God ordained before the world unto our glory" (I Cor. 2:7).[65] This mystery was of truths revealed only to those who possess the spirit:

> God has revealed to us through the Spirit. For the Spirit searches everything, even the depths of God. For what person knows a man's thoughts except the spirit of the man which is in him? So also no one comprehends the thoughts of God except the Spirit of God. Now we have received not the spirit of the world, but the Spirit which is from God, that we might understand the gifts bestowed upon us by God. And we impart this in words not taught by human wisdom but taught by the Spirit, interpreting spiritual truths to those who possess the Spirit.   I Cor. 2:10–13

In terms of cosmic metaphor, Paul understands the spiritual truths of Christianity to overcome and transcend the deterministic powers of this world;

> Formerly, when you did not know God, you were in bondage to beings that by nature are no gods; but now that you have come to know God, or rather to be known by God, how can you turn back again to the weak and beggarly elemental spirits [of the cosmos] whose slaves you want to be once more?
>   Gal. 4:8–9; also Col. 2:8

The reference to the "days, and months, and seasons, and years" that follows this passage indicates that the mythologized, that is, personified elements of the cosmos, refer to the astrological powers of the celestial realm that determine the calendar and rule over ritual observances (see also Col. 2:16).

Paul could recast the cosmic metaphor of determination as a temporal metaphor to include historical bondage to the requirements of law (Gal. 3:23–4:7), especially for his Jewish and Jewish-Christian audiences, and finally to include "philosophy and human traditions" generally (Col. 2:8). His consistent reference to the cross and to the suffering of Christ emphasizes his historical understanding of the redemptive event as well. Denying the temporal determinism of a Jewish past, Paul paradoxically attempted to appropriate for Christianity the possibilities of a future hope that was inherent in Jewish salvation history. Thus, he argued, the true heir of the promise to Abraham (Gen. 17:4–6) is Christianity (Gal. 3:29; 3:6–7; Rom. 4:16).

The gospel traditions further emphasized the redemptive act of Christ as historical event by providing the redeemer with a heroic and exemplary life. These later traditions extended the metaphor of cosmic transcendence to include that of the social, cultural, and political powers of this world as well: "Render to Caesar the things that are Caesar's, and to God the things that are God's" (Mark 12:17; Luke 20:25). That is to say, for Paul and for early Christianity generally, redemption was the transcendence of all deterministic powers and authority that had its locus within the cosmic realm, whether celestial or terrestrial.

Paul expressed his understanding of Christian existence in his central image for redemptive transcendence: freedom. "For freedom," he writes, "Christ has set us free" (Gal. 5:1; see also Gal. 2:4; 5:13; I Cor. 7:21; and II Cor. 3:17). For Paul, freedom from the deterministic powers of the world, whether historically manifest in Jewish law and philosophical tradition or cosmologically manifest in the astrological rule of the heavenly powers, was expressed by the image of the redemptive ascent/resurrection of Christ to the otherworld of the Father.

Appeal and Reaction

Mithraism was a religion of the camp, whether of the literally encamped military or of those encamped in their fixed social status as slaves, freedmen, and bureaucrats. Christianity, in contrast, was a more cosmopolitan movement whose democratic universalism offered a classless vision of the world. The early Christians were not the "ignorant," "stupid," "uneducated," "foolish," and "dishonorable" "slaves, women, and little children" that the Western tradition has romanticized since the second century (Origen, *C. Cel.* III, 44), but represented rather a cross-section of primarily urban society.[66]

Christian missionary activity had resulted in a network of these urban Christians. Unlike Apuleius's asinine Lucius, the new Christian could wander the labyrinthian world of late antiquity, from city to city, and always be received into the home and family of fellow Christians.[67] It was this spreading network of loyalties and allegiances, reminiscent of the situation that had led to the banning of the

Roman Bacchanalia three centuries earlier, upon which Rome cast an increasingly wary eye.

The earliest official reaction of Rome to Christianity is documented in a letter of Pliny the Younger, the newly appointed governor of Bithynia and Pontus, written in 111 C.E. to solicit the Emperor Trajan's advice on how to deal with this new religion:

> Having never been present at any trials of the Christians, I am unacquainted with the method and limits to be observed either in examining or punishing them. Whether any difference is to be made on account of age, or no distinction allowed between the youngest and the adult; whether repentance admits to a pardon, or if a man has been once a Christian it avails him nothing to recant; whether the mere profession Christianity, albeit without crimes, or only the crimes associated therewith are punishable—in all these points I am greatly doubtful.

> In the meanwhile, the method I have observed towards those who have been denounced to me as Christians is this: I interrogated them whether they were Christians; if they confessed it, I repeated the question twice again, adding the threat of capital punishment; if they still persevered, I ordered them to be executed. For whatever the nature of their creed might be, I could at least feel no doubt that contumacy and inflexible obstinacy deserved chastisement. There were others also possessed with the same infatuation, but being citizens of Rome, I directed them to be carried thither.

> These accusations spread (as is usually the case) from the mere fact of the matter being investigated and several forms of the mischief came to light. A placard was put up, without any signature, accusing a large number of persons by name. Those who denied they were, or had ever been, Christians, who repeated after me an invocation to the Gods, and offered adoration, with wine and frankincense, to your image, which I had ordered to be brought for that purpose, together with those of the Gods, and who finally cursed Christ— none of which acts, it is said, those who are really Christians can be forced into performing—these I thought it proper to discharge. Others who were named by that informer at first confessed themselves Christians, and then denied it; true, they had been of that persuasion but they had quitted it, some three years, others many years, and a few as many as twenty-five years ago. They all worshipped your statute and the images of the Gods, and cursed Christ.

> They affirmed, however, the whole of their guilt, or their error, was, that they were in the habit of meeting on a certain fixed day before it

was light, when they sang in alternate verses a hymn to Christ, as to a god, and bound themselves by a solemn oath, not to any wicked deeds, but never to commit any fraud, theft or adultery, never to falsify their word, nor deny a trust when they should be called upon to deliver it up; after which it was their custom to separate, and then reassemble to partake of food—but food of an ordinary and innocent kind. Even this practice, however, they had abandoned after the publication of my edict, by which, according to your orders, I had forbidden political associations. I judged it so much the more necessary to extract the real truth, with the assistance of torture, from two female slaves, who were styled deaconesses: but I could discover nothing more than depraved and excessive superstition.   *Tra.* 10, 96

Pliny's letter shows that Christianity was just beginning to attract official attention at the beginning of the second century and that there were no clear legal precedents for dealing with this new movement. As in the earlier case of the Bacchanalia, Pliny understood Christianity as a "political association" to be forbidden as a possible threat to the legitimate power of the state. Because the Christians obeyed even his ban against assembly, however, Pliny was at a loss to discover any law that had been broken or crime committed. Reduced to complaining about such Christian traits as their "contumacy and inflexible obstinacy," he concludes that, despite torture, "I could discover nothing more than depraved and excessive superstition."

For the Romans, *superstitio* was the name for beliefs and practices that were foreign or strange to them.[68] It was the way both Tacitus (*Ann.* 15, 44) and Suetonius (*Ner.* 16), friends and contemporaries of Pliny, also referred to Christianity.[69] Because Rome's criterion for true religion was ancient origin, her reactions against Christianity seem to have been based upon a political interpretation of its spreading sphere of influence, based, in turn, upon its novelty.

The growth and acceptance of Christianity during its first centuries, despite Pliny's judgment that "it seems possible, however, to check and cure it" (*Tra.* 10, 96), is much too complex for inclusion in this summary.[70] The nature of its success, however, is reflected by the reemergence in the fourth century of one of its most significant images, the "Cosmic Christ,"[71] by which Christians appealed to a faith based not only on revelation but also on a natural order of things.[72] As summarized by Basil of Caesarea (circa 330–379):

Before all those things which now attract our notice existed, God, after casting about in his mind and determining to bring into being

> that which had no being, imagined the world such as it ought to
> be, and created matter in harmony with the form which he wished
> to give it. . . . He welded all the diverse parts of the cosmos by
> links of indissoluble attachment and established between them so
> perfect a fellowship and harmony that the most distant, in spite of
> their distance, appeared united in one universal sympathy.
>
> *Hexaemeron* 2, 2[73]

This image claimed not only the recognized antiquity of Mosaic tradition but also Hellenistic cosmological theory. The assumed sympathetic harmony of world, which had been established by the speaking
(*logos*) of God (Gen. 1:1) and revealed to Moses, was now rendered
intelligible by a new speaking (*logos*) of God in the Christ event
(John 1:1).[74] This Christian appeal to *logos* both as divine reason
and the structure of cosmos overcame any view of existence as either
arbitrary (*tychē*) or deterministic (*heimarmenē*).[75]

Christianity offered a compromise between the world-transform-
ing Mysteries and world-denying gnostics: "be in the world but not of
it." It is sufficient to note that by the beginning of the fourth century,
the emperor Constantine found it prudent to link his reorganized and
renewed empire as closely as possible with this growing church. Unlike the pagan Mysteries, Christianity was the beneficiary of Theodosius's decrees and came to dominant Western culture.

Notes

1. William Arrowsmith (trans.), *The Complete Greek Tragedies,* vol.
IV, ed. David Grene and Richard Lattimore (Chicago: University of Chicago
Press, 1960).

2. See W. K. C. Guthrie, *The Greeks and Their Gods* (Boston: Beacon
Press, 1954), pp. 145–182.

3. Martin P. Nilsson, *The Dionysiac Mysteries of the Hellenistic and
Roman Age* (Lund, Sweden: C. W. K. Gleerup, 1957), p. 12.

4. Nilsson, p. 44.

5. Nilsson, p. 5.

6. Nilsson, pp. 7–8.

7. Nilsson, pp. 4, 115.

8. On the Dionysian elements in Euripides's drama, see E. R. Dodds,
Introduction to *The Bacchae,* 2nd ed. (Oxford: Oxford University Press,
1959).

9. Dodds, pp. ix–x.

10. This interpretation has been suggested by Rudolf Bultmann, *The Gospel of John: A Commentary,* trans. and gen. ed. G. R. Beasley-Murray, with R. W. N. Hoare and J. K. Riches (Philadelphia: Westminster Press, 1971), pp. 118–119.

11. Nilsson, pp. 21–37.

12. Nilsson, p. 37.

13. Nilsson, pp. 61–64.

14. Nilsson, p. 21.

15. For interpretations of Dionysian iconographic remains, see Nilsson, chap. VI, and C. Kerényi, *Dionysus: Archetypal Image of Indestructible Life,* trans. Ralph Manheim (Princeton, N.J.: Princeton University Press, 1976), chap. VI.

16. Harold R. Willoughby, *Pagan Regeneration: A Study of Mystery Initiations in the Graeco-Roman World* (Chicago: University of Chicago Press, 1974), chap. IV; W. K. C. Guthrie, *Orpheus and Greek Religion: A Study of the Orphic Movement* (New York: Norton, 1966), pp. 41–42, 194–195.

17. Guthrie, *Orpheus,* pp. 27–29.

18. Guthrie, *Orpheus,* pp. 29–31.

19. Guthrie, *Orpheus,* pp. 32–35.

20. Guthrie, *Orpheus,* pp. 35–39.

21. M. L. West, *The Orphic Poems* (Oxford: Clarendon Press, 1983), pp. 247–248.

22. West, p. 69.

23. Reconstructed by West, pp. 70–75.

24. Apostolos N. Athanassakis (trans.), *The Orphic Hymns,* (Missoula, Mont: Scholars Press, 1977).

25. "Mysteriosophy" is used by Ugo Bianchi to refer to "the whole complex of mythical-doctrinal notions generally known under the name of 'Orphism.' " He means by this term "a special manner of seeing the cosmos, man and the history of the gods: a manner which implies a . . . general mystic conception of life and of the cosmos, of its divine origins, of the perpetual and recurring cycle of changes which govern it, and also and in particular a doctrine of the soul as subject to an alternation of decay in this world subject to destiny (or to matter) and of final re-integration" (*The Greek Mysteries* [Leiden: E. J. Brill, 1976], p. 6).

26. West, pp. 2–3.

27. West, p. 3.

28. Larry J. Alderink, *Creation and Salvation in Ancient Orphism,* American Classical Studies 8 (Chico, Calif.: Scholars Press, 1981), chap. IV.

29. Alderink, p. 95.

30. Richard Reitzenstein, *Hellenistic Mystery-Religions: Their Basic Ideas and Significance,* trans. John E. Steely (Pittsburgh, Pa.: Pickwick Press, 1978), pp. 51–52, 62.

31. See "The Letter of Aristeas," in James H. Charlesworth (ed.), *The Old Testament Pseudepigrapha*, vol. 2 (Garden City, N.Y.: Doubleday, 1985), pp. 7–34.

32. Franz Cumont, *Astrology and Religion Among the Greeks and Romans*, trans. J.B. Baker (New York: Dover, 1960), pp. 84–85.

33. George Foot Moore, "Fate and Free Will in the Jewish Philosophies According to Josephus," *Harvard Theological Review* XXII (1929), pp. 371–389.

34. See the provocative discussion by Jonathan Z. Smith, *Map is Not Territory: Studies in the History of Religion* (Leiden: E. J. Brill, 1978), pp. 67–87.

35. Jewish canonical apocalypses include only the Book of Daniel (to which the New Testament adds only the Book of Revelation). A new translation of noncanonical apocalyptic texts is now edited by James H. Charlesworth, *The Old Testament Pseudepigrapha*, vol. 1: *Apocalyptic Literature and Testaments* (Garden City, N.Y.: Doubleday, 1983).

36. For the thesis of Jewish mysteries, see Erwin R. Goodenough, *By Light, Light* (Oxford: Oxford University Press, 1935), and the review by A. D. Nock, "The Question of Jewish Mysteries," in Zeph Stewart (ed.), *Essays on Religion and the Ancient World*, vol. I (Cambridge, Mass.: Harvard University Press, 1972), pp. 459–468.

37. Erwin R. Goodenough, *Jewish Symbols in the Greco-Roman Period*, 13 vols. (Princeton, N.J.: Princeton University Press, 1953–1968).

38. See the first-century C.E. Roman historian, Valerius Maximus I, 3, 2.

39. A. M. Harmon (trans.), *Lucian*, vol. IV, in the Loeb Classical Library (Cambridge, Mass.: Harvard University Press, 1925), p. 173.

40. Apollonius was compared to Jesus by Hierocles, a provincial governer under Diocletian, and was answered by Eusebius in *Contra Hieroclem*, trans. F. C. Conybeare, in the Loeb Classical Library (Cambridge, Mass.: Harvard University Press, 1912).

41. On Apollonius, see E. L. Bowie, "Apollonius of Tyana: Tradition and Reality," *Aufstieg und Niedergang der Römischen Welt* II, 16. 2 (Berlin and New York: Walter de Gruyter, 1978), pp. 1652–1699.

42. Franz Cumont, *The Mysteries of Mithra*, 2nd. ed., trans. Thomas J. McCormack (New York: Dover, 1956), fig. 1, p. 14.

43. Cumont's is the classic study that established for the twentieth century the thesis of Mithraism's Persian origin. Most recently, see the neo-Cumontian study by Reinhold Merkelbach, *Mithras* (Königstein/Ts.: Hain, 1984).

44. Roger Beck, "Mithraism Since Franz Cumont," *Aufstieg und Niedergang der Römischen Welt* II, 17. 4 (Berlin and New York: Walter de Gruyter, 1984), pp. 2002–2115.

45. See, for instance, Roger Beck, "Cautes and Cautopates: Some As-

tronomical Considerations," *Journal of Mithraic Studies* II (1977), pp. 1–17, and S. Insler, "A New Interpretation of the Bull-Slaying Motif," in M. B. de Boer and T. A. Edridge (eds.), *Hommages à Maarten J. Vermaseren* (Leiden: E. J. Brill, 1978), pp. 519–538.

46. See, for example, Michael P. Speidel, *Mithras-Orion: Greek Hero and Roman Army God* (Leiden: E. J. Brill, 1980); and David Ulansey, *Mithras and Perseus: Mithraic Astronomy and the Anatolian Perseus-Cult,* Doctoral Dissertation, Princeton University, 1984.

47. Speidel.

48. Ulansey, pp. 133–149.

49. Beck, pp. 2080–2081.

50. M. J. Vermaseren, *Mithras, The Secret God,* trans. Therese and Vincent Megaw (New York: Barnes & Noble, 1963), p. 177.

51. Porphyry, *The Cave of the Nymphs in the Odyssey,* trans. Seminar Classics 609, Arethusa Monographs 1 (Buffalo, N.Y.: Dept. of Classics, State University of New York, 1969).

52. R. L. Gordon, "The Sacred Geography of a *Mithraeum:* The Example of Sette Sfere," in *Journal of Mithraic Studies* I (1976), pp. 119–165.

53. A. S. Gedden (trans.), *Select Passages Illustrating Mithraism* (London: Society for Promoting Christian Knowledge, 1925), pp. 61–62. See also plates 22–28 (pp. 75–81) in Samuel Laeuchli (ed.), *Mithraism in Ostia* (Evanston, Ill.: Northwestern University Press, 1967), and discussion by Vermaseren, chap. 14.

54. The translation of "nymph" as Embryo is Merkelbach's, pp. 88–90.

55. Trans. M. J. Vermaseren, p. 178.

56. J. P. Kane, "The Mithraic Cult Meal in its Greek and Roman Environment," in John R. Hinnells (ed.), *Mithraic Studies: Proceedings of the First International Congress of Mithraic Studies,* vol. 2 (Manchester: Manchester University Press, 1975), pp. 313–351.

57. See the important and provocative article by R. L. Gordon, "Reality, evocation and boundary in the Mysteries of Mithras," *Journal of Mithraic Studies* III (1980), pp. 19–99.

58. *The "Mithras Liturgy",* ed. and trans. Marvin W. Meyer (Missoula, Mont.: Scholars Press, 1976).

59. Gordon, "Reality, evocation and boundary," pp. 44, 57.

60. Merkelbach, pp. 153–187.

61. On Tarsus, see William Mitchell Ramsay, *The Cities of St. Paul* (Grand Rapids, Mich.: Baker Book House, 1949), pp. 85–244. On the Cilician origins of Mithraism, see Plutarch, *Vit. Pomp. 24,* and Ulansey, pp. 150–168.

62. Gregory Dix, *The Shape of the Liturgy* (London: Adam and Charles Black, 1960), chap. III, esp. pp. 41–42.

63. On the common elements of the Hellenistic cosmic myth, see Jonathan Z. Smith, pp. 61–62, and bibliography, p. 62, n. 68.

64. Gershom G. Scholem, *Major Trends in Jewish Mysticism* 3rd ed. (New York: Schocken Books, 1961), pp. 50, 54.

65. King James translation.

66. Wayne A. Meeks, *The First Urban Christians: The Social World of the Apostle Paul* (New Haven, Conn.: Yale University Press, 1983), pp. 51–53, 73.

67. H. Idris Bell, *Cults and Creeds in Graeco-Roman Egypt* (Chicago: Ares, 1975), p. 105; Meeks, pp. 109–110.

68. Robert L. Wilken, *The Christians as the Romans Saw Them* (New Haven, Conn.: Yale University Press, 1984), pp. 50–54.

69. Wilkens, pp. 49–50.

70. For a survey of traditional perspectives and contributing factors in the coming to dominance of Christianity, see John G. Gager, *Kingdom and Community: The Social World of Early Christianity* (Englewood Cliffs, N.J.: Prentice-Hall, 1975), chap. 5.

71. Jaroslav Pelikan, *Jesus Through the Centuries: His Place in the History of Culture* (New Haven, Conn.: Yale University Press, 1985), chap. 5, pp. 57–70.

72. Pelikan, p. 64.

73. Cited by Pelikan, p. 65.

74. Pelikan, p. 59.

75. Pelikan, p. 64.

Selected Bibliography

The Myth of Dionysus

Euripides, *The Bacchae,* trans. William Arrowsmith in David Grene and Richard Lattimore (eds.), *The Complete Greek Tragedies,* vol. IV (Chicago: University of Chicago Press, 1960).

E. R. Dodds (intro. and commentary), *The Bacchae,* 2nd ed. (Oxford: Oxford University Press, 1959).

Hesiod, The Homeric Hymns and Homerica, rev. ed., trans. Hugh G. Evelyn-White, in the Loeb Classical Library (Cambridge, Mass.: Harvard University Press, 1936).

Studies of Dionysus

C. Kerényi, *Dionysus: Archetypal Image of Indestructible Life,* trans. Ralph Manheim (Princeton, N.J.: Princeton University Press, 1976).

Martin P. Nilsson, *The Dionysiac Mysteries of the Hellenistic and Roman Age,* (Lund, Sweden: C. W. K. Gleerup, 1957).

Walter F. Otto, *Dionysus: Myth and Cult,* trans. Robert B. Palmer (Bloomington, Ind.: Indiana University Press, 1965).

Orpheus

Larry J. Alderink, *Creation and Salvation in Ancient Orphism,* American Classical Studies 8 (Chico, Calif.: Scholars Press, 1981).
Apostolos N. Athanassakis (trans.), *The Orphic Hymns* (Missoula, Mont.: Scholars Press, 1977).
Robert Eisler, *Orpheus—The Fisher: Comparative Studies in Orphic and Early Christian Cult Symbolism* (London: J. M. Watkins, 1921).
W. K. C. Guthrie, *Orpheus and Greek Religion: A Study of the Orphic Movement* (New York: Norton, 1966).
G. R. S. Mead, *Orpheus* (New York: Barnes & Noble, 1965).
M. L. West, *The Orphic Poems* (Oxford: Clarendon Press, 1983).
Walter Wili, "The Orphic Mysteries and the Greek Spirit," in Joseph Campbell (ed.), *The Mysteries: Papers from the Eranos Yearbooks,* vol. 2, trans. Ralph Manheim and R. F. C. Hull (New York: Pantheon Books, 1955).

Hellenistic Judaism

Erwin R. Goodenough, *Jewish Symbols in the Greco-Roman Period,* 13 vols. (Princeton, N.J.: Princeton University Press, 1953–1968).
Martin Hengel, *Judaism and Hellenism: Studies in their Encounter in Palestine during the Early Hellenistic Period,* 2 vols., trans. John Bowden (Philadelphia: Fortress Press, 1974), includes a comprehensive bibliography.
Victor Tcherikover, *Hellenistic Civilization and the Jews,* trans. S. Applebaum (New York: Atheneum, 1970).

Josephus and Philo

Erwin R. Goodenough, *An Introduction to Philo Judaeus,* 2nd ed. (Oxford: Basil Blackwell, 1962).
Samuel Sandmel, *Philo of Alexandria* (New York: Oxford University Press, 1979).
H. St. John Thackeray, *Josephus: The Man and the Historian* (New York: KTAV Publishing House, 1967).

The Dead Sea Scrolls

Frank Moore Cross, Jr., *The Ancient Library of Qumran and Biblical Studies,* rev. ed. (Garden City, NY: Doubleday, 1961).

Theodor H. Gaster (intro. and notes), *The Dead Sea Scriptures in English Translation* (Garden City, N.Y.: Doubleday, 1956).

G. Vermes, *The Dead Sea Scrolls in English* (Baltimore: Penguin Books, 1962).

Jewish Wisdom Literature

James L. Crenshaw, *Old Testament Wisdom: An Introduction* (Atlanta, Ga.: John Knox Press, 1981).

Donn F. Morgan, *Wisdom in the Old Testament Traditions* (Atlanta, Ga.: John Knox Press, 1981).

O. S. Rankin, *Israel's Wisdom Literature: Its Bearing on Theology and the History of Religion* (Edinburgh: T. & T. Clark, 1936).

Helmer Ringgren, *Word and Wisdom* (Lund, Sweden: Ohlssons, 1947).

Gerhard von Rad, *Wisdom in Israel,* trans. James D. Marton (London: SCM Press, 1972).

Sabazios

Sherman E. Johnson, "The Present State of Sabazios Research", *Aufstieg und Niedergang der Römischen Welt* II, 17. 3 (Berlin and New York: Walter de Gruyter, 1984), pp. 1583–1613.

W. O. E. Oesterly, "The Cult of Sabazios," in S. H. Hooke (ed.), *The Labyrinth: Further Studies in the Relation Between Myth and Ritual in the Ancient World,* (London: Society for Promoting Christian Knowledge and New York: Macmillan, 1935), pp. 113–158.

Mithraism: Texts

A. S. Gedden (trans.), *Select Passages Illustrating Mithraism* (London: Society for Promoting Christian Knowledge, 1925).

Lucian, *Alexander the False Prophet,* trans. A. M. Harmon, in the Loeb Classical Library, vol. IV (Cambridge, Mass.: Harvard University Press, 1925).

Porphyry, *The Cave of the Nymphs in the Odyssey,* trans. Seminar Classics 609, Arethusa Monographs 1 (Buffalo, N.Y.: Dept. of Classics, State University of New York, 1969).

Mithraism: Studies

Roger Beck, "Mithraism Since Franz Cumont," *Aufstieg und Niedergang der Römischen Welt* II, 17. 4 (Berlin and New York: Walter de Gruyter, 1984), pp. 2002–2115, is a complete bibliographical essay.

L. A. Campbell, *Mithraic Iconography and Ideology* (Leiden: E. J. Brill,

1968) is even more thoroughgoing than Cumont in arguing for the Persian origins of Mithraism.

Franz Cumont, *The Mysteries of Mithra,* 2nd ed., trans. Thomas J. McCormack (New York: Dover, 1956).

Reinhold Merkelbach, *Mithras,* Königstein/Ts.: Hain, 1984.

M. J. Vermaseren, *Mithras, The Secret God,* trans. Therese and Vincent Megaw (New York: Barnes & Noble, 1963), is essentially an update of Cumont in light of new discoveries.

David Ulansey, *Mithras and Perseus: Mithraic Astronomy and the Anatolian Perseus-Cult,* Doctoral Dissertation, Princeton University, 1984.

Christianity

Stephen Benko, *Pagan Rome and the Early Christians,* (Bloomington, Ind.: Indiana University Press, 1984).

Ramsay MacMullen, *Christianizing the Roman Empire* (A.D. *100–400*) (New Haven, Conn.: Yale University Press, 1984).

Wayne A. Meeks, *The First Urban Christians: The Social World of the Apostle Paul* (New Haven, Conn.: Yale University Press, 1983).

James M. Robinson and Helmut Koester, *Trajectories Through Early Christianity* (Philadelphia: Fortress Press, 1971).

Robert L. Wilken, *The Christians as the Romans Saw Them* (New Haven, Conn.: Yale University Press, 1984).

Apollonius

Ewen Lyall Bowie, "Apollonius of Tyana: Tradition and Reality", *Aufstieg und Niedergang der Römischen Welt* II, 16. 2 (Berlin and New York: Walter de Gruyter, 1978), pp. 1652–1699.

5

Late Hellenistic Gnosis

From the first century B.C.E., a remarkable new figure is identifiable in the Hellenistic world, the masculine redeemer. Whereas "savior" designated any agent of transformation, divine or mortal, male or female, "redeemer" was reserved exclusively for divine masculine agents of a transcendent Father God. The Mysteries had assumed a terrestrial deficiency that the universal soteriological goddess transformed for her initiates, thereby maintaining an essentially positive view of the cosmos. Mithraism had offered its followers a revaluation of the structures of their everyday existence based upon a ritual reorientation toward and integration of the total cosmos. Similarly, Christianity had rejected the everyday claims of this world but, unlike Mithraism, set out to convert the entire world to its catholic ideal. Increasingly, however, a gnostic alternative radically revalued this world as something to be rejected completely and transcended.

Cosmic Revaluation

The seeds of a late Hellenistic revaluation of the cosmos were present already in earlier views of the natural order. Astrology, for example (and by analogy all systems for ordering terrestrial existence), was a positive technique for overcoming fortune through knowledge of an assumed sympathetic cosmic order. But increasingly, this order itself came to be seen as antipathetic, imposing upon human existence an implacable destiny. The cosmic structure, traditionally imaged in terms of the capricious feminine principle, became identified exclusively with the unfavorable side of the feminine. This oppressive feminine cosmos actively encompassed the fallen and demonic powers that acted not only to enslave humans, but also to exclude the antithetical masculine god.

The deterministic rule of the cosmos was known as *heimarmenē,* destiny or oppressive fate. A feminine noun, this abstract image of late Hellenistic existence was never personified as was Tyche/Fortuna—except by denial. For example, the Christian convert and apologist Clement of Alexandria, who wrote late in the second century C.E. that the Romans believed Fortuna to be the greatest deity (*Protr.* IV), sarcastically rejects *heimarmenē* as a goddess (*Protr.* X).

The number of controlling powers corresponded to some variation on a cosmological/astrological system, such as the seven planets of the Ptolemaic system, the five dark planets excluding the sun and the moon, or the twelve zodiacal rings, up to a calendrical 365. As formulated in terms of the planetary spheres by the second century C.E. opening tractate of the *Corpus Hermeticum,*

> God . . . created seven Rulers [i.e., the planets] which encircle the world perceived through the senses. Their government is called Destiny [*Heimarmenē*]. *CH* I, 9[1]

But the number of powers per se were less important than their role as agents of cosmic determinism.

The incarcerating powers of the cosmos were extended from the enveloping spheres of the stars and planets to the embodied nature of individual existence, following the principle of macrocosmic/microcosmic parallelism. Planets, earth, and flesh all shared matter in common. Consequently, the deficiency of all existence was mythologized as a cosmogonic/anthropogonic fall into matter from a realm of divine spirit beyond the cosmic confines. For late Hellenistic anticosmism, the possibility of soteriological transformation no longer existed within the fallen confines of the cosmos.

At about the same time, the astronomer and astrologer Hipparchus (circa 190 until after 126 B.C.E.) had discovered the procession of the equinoxes.[2] Although not mentioned by other astronomers until the second century C.E., when Ptolemy described it in his *Algamest,*[3]

Hipparchus's discovery must have been known in at least some astronomically oriented circles by the first century C.E.[4] From the geocentric perspective of Hellenistic cosmology, Hipparchus had discovered a movement of the fixed stars themselves. Any activity by this stellar sphere of the cosmos challenged the prevailing view of a stable container of the contained cosmos, hence the empirical basis for any final cosmic order. If the stars themselves were transitory, it followed that the cosmos in its totality must be ruled by a relative rather than an absolute natural order, and finally by chance. Whether understood as external forces of nature that ordered but entombed man in an inescapably determined condition, or as demonic personae united in a dance of cosmic chaos, the cosmic spheres increasingly were understood to represent a tyranny of this-worldly existence.

The mythocosmic reformulation of this-worldly existence as completely negative established both the condition and the governing image for a renunciation of any claim by this world and its social, political, or cosmic powers upon human existence. The recognition and acceptance of these conditions cast their knower radically upon the inner resources of the knowing self.

The true self, understood to be spiritually consubstantial with an otherworldly sacrality, could be redeemed and the stains left from its contamination by matter removed only by a reunion with its transcendent origin. To transcend cosmic deficiency was to overcome the binding power of the cosmos itself. As expressed in the Christian imagery of the Gnostic Theodotus:

> Therefore a strange and new star arose doing away with the old astral decree, shining with a new unearthly light, which revolved on a new path of salvation, as the Lord himself, men's guide, who came down to earth to transfer from Fate [*heimarmenē*] to his providence those who believed in Christ.   *Exc. Thdt.* 74, 2[5]

Only the transcendent masculine principle provided an alternative to the feminine nature of fallen matter.

The Hellenistic soteriological pattern of transformation familiar to the Mysteries, then, was replaced by a later Hellenistic redemptive pattern of transcendence. Through the intervening activity of a masculine redeemer, the consubstantial soul might transcend the fallen feminine structures of matter in order to be reunited with its otherworldly divine Father. Together, a negative feminine cosmic determinism or anomie, spirit or soul as a portion of the divine fallen into and imprisoned by this dark and fallen matter, and a transcendent masculine redemptive agent, antithetic to matter but sympathetic with soul, were the characteristic traits of gnostic discourse.

Gnosticism

Gnostic thought exemplified the late-Hellenistic strategy of radical personal existence. Its view of an inner or spiritual redemption was largely intellectual, to judge from its emphasis on writing[6] and on the quality of the surviving texts.[7] Its most articulate spokesmen worked out of such cosmopolitan centers as Edessa, Antioch, Ephesus, Alexandria, and Rome.[8]

Gnostic thought was rarely if ever institutionalized as an autonomous movement. Rather, it was articulated through such existing religious and philosophical traditions as Jewish apocalyptic and wisdom speculations, Orphism, Middle Platonism, and especially Christianity.[9] As a class, Gnostics understood themselves to be superior to nongnostic understandings of their various traditions.

Only by assuming its autonomy has Gnosticism been identifiable as a discrete "cluster of attributes."[10] This assumption was established by the Christian Fathers: Justin and Irenaeus in the second century, and Hippolytus, Clement of Alexandria, Origen, and Tertullian in the third, who understood Gnosticism, from their perspective of an ecclesiastical politics of orthodoxy, as Christian heresy.[11]

According to the Church Fathers, Gnosticism originated with Simon Magus (Acts 8:9–24) and included the followers of some of the most well-known names of early heresiological literature: Menander, Saturninus, Carpocrates, Cerinthus, Cerdo, Marcion, Basilides, and Valentinus (Irenaeus, *Haer.* I, 22–31). The understanding of Gnosticism was considerably broadened with the discovery in 1945 of thirteen codices containing fifty-one primary gnostic texts from the late Hellenistic period, which had been buried in the upper Nile region of Egypt near the town of Nag Hammadi. The discovery of these Nag Hammadi codices (*NHC*) contributes enormously to an understanding of both Christian and non-Christian gnostic spirituality.[12]

Christian and Non-Christian Gnosis

A growing consensus of scholarship, based upon the Nag Hammadi discovery, argues for the existence of a non-Christian, Jewish Gnosticism.[13] One group of texts suggests, for example, a loose commentary tradition based upon a mythologizing interpretation of Seth, the third son of Adam referred to in Genesis 4:25 and 5:1–3, and posits true Gnostics as the spiritual seed of Seth, the revealing redeemer of gnosis.[14] As related in the *Aprocryphon of John,* one of the Nag Hammadi texts, after the Invisible Spirit had placed Adam on the first aeon "with the mighty one, the Autogenes, the Christ,"

> he placed his son Seth on the second aeon. . . . And in the third aeon the seed [descendants] of Seth was placed. . . . And the souls of the saints were placed (there). And in the fourth aeon the souls were placed of those who do not know the Pleroma and who did not repent at once, but who persisted for a while [seeking] and repented afterwards.   *NHC* II, 1, 9, 11–25

Such references defining Gnostics as those who belong to an elect race of Seth is the central feature of a Sethian Gnosticism.[15] A pre-gnostic Jewish speculation on Seth seems to have preceded a Jewish-gnostic Sethianism and was then further interpreted into a Christian-gnostic Sethianism.[16]

Perhaps the most important example of a Christian Gnosticism was the tradition of Valentinus—at least to judge from the attention given it by the early heresiologists. Valentinus was a mid-second-century Christian who, according to Tertullian, "broke with the church of the true faith" after he was passed over for the office of bishop in favor of another (*Adv. Valent.* IV). According to an account by Hippolytus (*Haer.* VI, 37), Valentinius had encountered and received revelation from an infant child who claimed to be the Logos. This relatively late account from the early third century preserves the Valentinian claim of revelatory origin, made by all Gnostic traditions, although Valentinus apparently was more influenced by the important *Apocryphon of John.*[17]

Valentinian Christianity was the most coherent of the gnostic movements although it never developed any authoritative canon or organized church. It survived until the fifth century c.e. as a loose tradition of individual teachers.[18] As Irenaus reports of these teachers,

> every one of them generates something new, day by day, according to his ability; for no one is deemed "perfect," who does not develop among them some mighty fictions.   *Haer.* I, 18, 1[19]

Gnostic thinkers sought to compile a spiritual inventory of the true self in terms of cosmological speculation, an area of reflection that had been slighted by Hellenistic philosophies in favor of ethical concerns. They opposed cosmic or spatial metaphors for existence to the predominantly historical or temporal scheme of things championed by "orthodox" Jewish and Christian thought.[20] This hierarchical framework for self-understanding facilitated a concern with self-reflective insight as opposed to the historical categories of past and future with their view of a temporal order.

The cosmologies of both Sethian and Valentinian myth were articulated in terms of the cosmogonic fall of Sophia, the feminine principle of gnostic myth. As expressed in the *Apocryphon of John,* the chief archon

> made a plan with his authorities, which are his powers, and they committed together adultery with Sophia, and bitter fate [*heimarmenē*] was begotten through them, which is the last of the terrible bonds. And it is of a sort that they are dreadful to each other. And it is harder and stronger than she with whom the gods are united and the angels and the demons and all the generations until this day. For from that fate came forth every sin and injustice and blasphemy and the chain of forgetfulness and ignorance and every difficult command and serious sins and great fear. And thus the whole creation was made blind, in order that they may not know God who is above all of them. And because of the chain of forgetfulness their sins were hidden. For they are bound with measures and times and moments, since it (fate) is lord over everything.
>
> *NHC* II, 1, 28, 11–32

Sophia was the willing participant in the adulterous union that produced *heimarmenē* and its fallen and oppressive rule over human existence. Similarly, Irenaeus (*Haer.* I, 1–2) reports that in Valentinian myth the curiosity of Sophia, the youngest and last of the Aeons, to know the glory of the primal Forefather precipitated her fall and the ensuing cosmogony.

According to the Valentinian myth as reported by Irenaeus, the original error of Sophia resulted in her giving birth to the Demiurge, identified by the Valentinians with the creator god of this world worshipped by Jews and Christians. This world and man, then, were created out of ignorance and conceit. The Valentinian cosmogony elaborated a complex devolution from divine to human, from spiritual to material, from light to dark, from knowledge to ignorance,

from unified at-homeness to alienated homelessness. Like the characteristic duplicity of Tyche/Fortuna, Sophia also has two sides. Her
error resulted in her separation into a higher Sophia, who is purified
and restored to her divine place through the intervention of the masculine redeemer, and a lower Sophia, who continued to endure a
fallen existence.

Although the Gnostics apparently accorded equal status to women
in worldly activities,[21] their cosmological view finally necessitated a
view of the feminine principle as inferior. As expressed in the Sethian
tractate, *Zostrianos*:

> Flee from the madness and the bondage of femininity, and choose
> for yourselves the salvation of masculinity. You have come not [to
> suffer], but to escape your bondage.   *NHC* VIII, I, 131, 5–10

And the Valentinian *Gospel of Philip* stated:

> When Eve was still in Adam death did not exist. When she was
> separated from him death came into being.
> *NHC* II, 3, 68, 22–26

However mythologized, the sovereignty of the feminine principle was
revalued in gnostic thought primarily as a fallen rule over a fallen
cosmos. Redemption was effected by the redeemer, the masculine
representative of the otherworldly Forefather.

Gnostic Seeking

By their own accounts, adherents of the various gnostic traditions
understood themselves as seekers of a higher spiritual knowledge
than that offered by this worldly cults and philosophical teachings. As
expressed by Jesus in the Christian-gnostic *Gospel of Thomas,* "let
him who seeks continue seeking until he finds" (*NHC* II, 2, 32, 15–
16). This motif of gnostic "seeking" replaced the geographical "wandering" motif of the Mysteries with a spiritualized, inner quest.

The theme of spiritual seeking in a fallen world is discussed in the
opening lines of *The Treatise on Resurrection,* one of the Nag
Hammadi texts:

> Some there are, my son Rheginos, who want to learn much. They
> have this goal when they are occupied with questions whose answer

is lacking. If they succeed with these, they usually think very highly of themselves. But I do not think that they have stood within the Word of Truth. They seek rather their own rest, which we have received through our Savior, our Lord Christ. We received it (Rest) when we knew the truth and rested ourselves upon it. But since you ask us pleasantly what is proper concerning the resurrection, I am writing you (to say) that it is necessary. To be sure, many are lacking faith in it, but there are a few who find it.

NHC I, 4, 43, 25–44, 10

The author of this text distinguishes between two kinds of seekers. The first include those "who want to learn much" and consequently "are occupied [in Greek, *zetema,* meaning that which is sought; from *zeteō,* to seek] with questions whose answer is lacking." These false seekers are further characterized as seeking "their own rest," a gnostic redemptive image. This kind of self-seeking after redemption is specifically identified as characteristic of philosophy and is held to be deficient (*NHC* I, 4, 46, 3–13). The epistemological quest has no redemptive answer because philosophy is considered to be a human tradition of this world, as it is by Paul (Gal. 1:2; see also Col. 2:8), who is authoritatively cited in this treatise (*NHC* I, 4, 45, 24–28).

The intellectual seeking of philosophy is contrasted with a spiritual seeking, a "received" discovery, mediated through a tradition of revealed gnosis. This spiritual seeking of the Gnostics is exemplified by that of Rheginos, the addressee of the text, who is counted among the elect "few." It assumes an innate gnosis requisite to true knowledge:

We are elected to salvation and redemption since we are predestined from the beginning not to fall into the foolishness of those who are without knowledge.   *NHC* I, 4, 46:25–29

Gnostic seeking was equivalent to remembering one's forgotten but original and true self. As Clement of Alexander wrote, "It is then the greatest of all lessons to know one's self" (*Paedegogus* III; see also *Gospel of Thomas, NHC* II, 32, 25–33,2). And in the words of the well-known passage from the *Excerpts of Theodotus* preserved by Clement of Alexandria, true gnosis is

the knowledge of who we were, and what we have become, where we were or where we were placed, whither we hasten, from what we are redeemed, what birth is and what rebirth.

Exc. Thdt. 78, 2

In other words, the structure of true gnosis involved knowledge of cosmogony/cosmology ("where we were or where we were placed . . . whither we hasten, from what we are redeemed"), anthropogony/anthropology ("who we were, and what we have become"), and redemption (birth and rebirth).

Because Gnostics imaged the cosmogonic fall as a devolution of spirit into matter, or even as an attack upon the realm of the spirit by the realm of matter, they understood a true spiritual self similarly embattled by and ensnared in matter/flesh. Consequently, they distinguished two modes of human existence; the *pneumatikoi* (from the Greek *pneuma,* meaning spirit), or the spiritual ones, and the *hylēkoi* (from the Greek *hylē,* meaning matter), or the fallen, material ones. Some further differentiated hylic existence into the *sarkikoi* (from the Greek *sarx,* meaning flesh), the embodied ones, and the *psychikoi* (from the Greek *psychē,* meaning soul), or the embodied ones who, although fallen, were characterized nevertheless by their "seeking" and thus open to redemption.

The myth of descent into this world by the masculine redeemer, the spiritual counterpart of the embodied soul, and his revelation of true gnosis constituted the mythological basis for a reversal of cosmic and anthropological fall and thereby the basis for a rejection of the claims of this world. In gnostic thought existence in a fallen and alien cosmos was subject finally to redemption, a triumph of individual hope over a pervasive cosmic despair.[22]

Gnostic Cult

Gnostics were in principle anti-cult.[23] Irenaeus writes that the Valentinians

> reject all . . . practices, and maintain that the mystery of the unspeakable and invisible power ought not to be performed by the visible and corruptible creatures, nor should that of those [beings] who are inconceivable, and incorporeal, and beyond the reach of sense, [be performed] by such as are the objects of sense, and possessed of a body. These hold that the knowledge of the unspeakable Greatness is itself perfect redemption. For since both defect and passion flowed from ignorance, the whole substance of what was thus formed is destroyed by knowledge: and therefore knowledge is the redemption of the inner man. This, however, is not of a corporeal nature, for the body is corruptible; nor is it animal, since

the animal soul is the fruit of a defect, and is, as it were, the abode of the spirit. The redemption must therefore be of a spiritual nature; for they affirm that the inner and spiritual man is redeemed by means of knowledge, and that they, having acquired the knowledge of all things, stand thenceforth in need of nothing else. This, then, is the true redemption. *Haer.* I, 21, 4

The discovery of spiritual self-knowledge was the redemptive ritual common to the various gnostic movements. Knowledge of the gnostic revelation itself, often communicated and preserved in writing, was the redemptive call sufficient to awaken the matter-burdened spirit to its true spiritual self. Although in practice there may have been some gnostic rites, these were a function of the traditions in terms of which gnostic thought was articulated—as for example, the Christian Gnosticism of Valentinus. It remained for the third-century c.e. followers of Mani to develop the first gnostic church.

Manichaeism

Mani (216–276) was from Southern Mesopotamia, of Persian parents. His father was a member of the Elkesaites, a Jewish-Christian gnostic baptist community. Mani clamed revelatory origin for his teaching, a claim characteristic of gnostic thinkers. According to the *Cologne Mani Codex* (*CMC*),[24] Mani received his first revelation following several preparatory visions during his childhood (*CMC* 2–14):

> [When] I was twenty[-four] years old, [in] the year in which Dariardaxar, the King of Persia, subdued the city Atra, also in which his son Sapores, the King, crowned himself with the grand diadem, in the month of Pharmouthi, on the eighth day of the lunar month, the most blessed Lord was greatly moved with compassion for me, called me into his grace, and immediately sent to me [from there my] Twin, [appearing in] great [glory]. *CMC* 18

> When, then, he (the Twin) came, he delivered, separated, and pulled me away from the midst of that Law in which I was reared. In this way he called, chose, drew, and severed me from their midst . . . , drawing [me to the divine] side. *CMC* 20

In an elaborate passage, reminiscent of Theodotus's famous summary of gnosis (*Exc. Thdt.* 78, 2), the Twin then instructs Mani concerning

who I am, what my body is, in what way I have come, how my arrival
into this world took place, who I am of the ones most renowned for
their eminence, how I was begotten into this fleshly body, by what
woman I was delivered and born according to the flesh, and by whose
[passion] I was engendered. . . . and how [. . .] came into being;
and who my Father on high is; or in what way, severed from him, I
was sent out according to his purpose. . . .

(the Twin showed Mani) the secrets and [visions] and the perfec-
tions of my Father; and concerning me, who I am, and who my
inseparable Twin is; moreover, concerning my soul, which exists as
the soul of all the worlds, both what it itself is and how it came to be.
Beside these, he revealed to me the boundless heights and the un-
fathomable depths; he showed [me] all.   *CMC* 21–23

Following his vision, Mani broke with the baptist group of his father
and began widespread missionary activity on his own behalf. King
Shapur I of Babylonia became his follower, and with this imperial
patronage, Manichaeism flourished. However, Bahram, a later King
of Babylonia, imprisoned Mani; he died in prison, a martyr according
to his followers.[25]

Mani had traveled east to India, and Manichaeism reached China
by the seventh century. It survived in the East until the thirteenth
century, when it was finally suppressed by the Mongols. Mani had
sent his emissaries to the West, and Manichaeism reached Egypt and
the Roman Empire by the fourth century, officially surviving into the
sixth. Manichaean themes reappeared in the Middle Ages among the
tenth-century Bogomites and the twelfth-century Albigensians, and
its influence is still detectable in Christian theology.[26]

Mani taught a radical ontological dualism unlike the devolved
dualism of Valentinian gnosis.[27] As Augustine charged the Manichaean Faust, "you teach that there are two principles, one good and
one evil," which are identified with God and Matter (*Contra Faustum*
XXI, 1).[28] This ethical dualism of God and Matter expressed a primordial cosmic dualism of Light and Dark. Because of his purity and
complete lack of any maleficence, God was unable to defend himself
against the hostility of Darkness, whose attack provided the external
cause of cosmogony.

In a first creation, God called forth the Primal Man to be the
defendant of Light. His voluntary descent into Matter, by which he
was seemingly defeated and imprisoned by Darkness, introduced an
element of Light into Darkness. In a second creation, God called

forth the Living Spirit, or Demiurge, for the redemption of the Primal Man. The Living Spirit descended to the threshold of Darkness and with a loud call awakened Primal Man from his stupor. Responding to this call, Primal Man was raised up victorious from the powers of Darkness and with the Living Spirit returned to his otherworldly origin.

In his ascent the Primal Man left behind his soul, particles of Light still mixed in Darkness. The Living Spirit created the visible cosmos as a mechanism for separating and rescuing these residual Light particles. From the least contaminated particles, he fashioned the solar and lunar celestial vessels of Light. From the slightly mixed Light, he fashioned the less brilliant stars. From the elements of Darkness, he made the planets and the earth. In the Manichaean system, therefore, the cosmos represented an ascending hierarchy from the darkness of the earth itself to the brilliance of the sun.

From a third creation emerged the Messenger, whose task was to rescue the remaining entrapped and mixed particles of Light. He set in motion the celestial lights, whose revolutions established guides for the entrapped particles below and whose spheres established support and way stations for the final ascent and recollection of those particles.

In a counterattack against God's attempts to rescue the abandoned Light particles, Darkness fashioned Adam and Eve, trapping the remaining particles of Light in their person and thus in darkness and matter. The abandoned soul of the Primal Man had become effectively embodied in a corporeal existence, and the cosmic drama became projected into human history.

Once again, God sent the Messenger through his emanation of the Luminous Jesus to bring revelatory gnosis to man. In the form of a serpent, Luminous Jesus caused Adam to eat of the Tree of Knowledge (gnosis). This scene of gnostic revelation to the first man by Christ, the suffering Primal Man, established the prototype for individual redemption. Every soul that responded to the gnostic call would ascend from its corporeal mixture with matter into the cosmic hierarchy of increasing light to reunite with its consubstantial and otherworldly source. The long cosmic process of redemption would be completed with the final separation of Light and Dark, indicating the defeat of the active and aggressive nature of the powers of Darkness and the restoration of the entire Light-unity.

Manichaeism differed from earlier expressions of gnosis not only in its ontological dualism but also in its imaging of the fall in terms of Primal Man, whose passion and redemption was nevertheless the mythological center of Manichaeism. Although the evil of Darkness into which he fell was introduced into human history by Eve's seduction of Adam, the Manichaean cosmic drama of fall and redemption turned predominantly on masculine activity, a central theme it shares with the hermetic literature.

The Hermetic Tradition

The *Corpus Hermeticum* is a collection of texts from the second and third centuries of our era that survived from a more extensive literature (see, for example, *NHC* VI, 6). Reflecting the generalized spiritual orientation of late Hellenistic gnosis rather than a tradition in any organized sense, these sometimes contradictory texts share only their claim to a common source of revelation, Hermes Trismegistus. This "thrice-great" Hermes was the Greek designation for the Egyptian deity Thoth or Tat, the messenger and scribe of the gods. In most of the texts his revelations are presented as a dialogue with one of three pupils: Tat, Asclepius, or Ammon. According to Augustine (*De Civitate Dei* VII, 26), Asclepius was the grandson of the great Greek god of the same name, and Tat was likewise the grandson of his divine namesake (the Roman deity Mercurius, the same as the Greek god Hermes).

The hermetic texts are often cited as examples of the extent of late Hellenistic syncretism, for they exhibit traits of magic, astrology, alchemy, Platonism and Stoicism, and the Mysteries, as well as Judaism and gnostic thought. Such influences are not arbitrary borrowings but express the systemic assumptions of the late Hellenistic age generally: the Ptolemaic delineation of a hierarchical cosmos under the rule of *heimarmenē,* the sympathetic parallel between macrocosm and microcosm, the attendant understanding of the consubstantial nature of all existent entities, the devolved or fallen feminine nature of reality, and the masculine redemptive possibility of cosmic and temporal reversal and thus of the effects of fall by means of a spiritual participation in the golden antiquity of origin.

Hermeticism may be illustrated from the *Poimandres,* the first and most well-known of the tractates. The *Poimandres* opens with the visionary account of an unnamed seeker:

> One day, when I began to reflect on existence, and my thoughts had soared, and my bodily senses were held down like people heavy with

sleep through surfeit of food or physical exhaustion, it seemed to me
that a giant creature of immeasurable dimensions approached, called
me by name, and said: "What do you wish to hear and to see and to
learn and to know with understanding?" And I said: "Who are you
then?" "I," he said, "am Poimandres, the Nous (Intellect) of the
Absolute Sovereignty. I know what you wish, and I am with you
everywhere." And I said: "I desire to learn the things that exist, to
understand their nature and to know God. How much do I desire to
hear!" Again he said to me: "Hold fast in your mind what you wish to
learn and I will teach you." *CH* I, 1–3

The passage is characterized by a dualistic distinction between the
corporeality of the "bodily senses" and Nous, the inner-thought or
intellect of the seer, which soars aloft to receive spiritual revelation.
The redemptive knowledge of "the things that exist," of their nature,
and of (what was the same thing) the knowledge of God, is revealed
in this noncorporeal vision by Poimandres. As the visionary reflects
at the conclusion of the revelation,

the sleep of the body became the wakefulness of the soul, the
closing of my eyes became true vision and my silence became
pregnant with the good, and the expression of my words the birth
of good things. And all this happened to me since I had received it
from my Intellect, that is from Poimandres, the Logos of the Absolute Sovereignty. *CH* I, 30

That is to say, Poimandres is the mythologized or projected consub-
stantiality of the human soul and God, the mediating Nous of the
mind and of the Absolute Sovereignty. When the Nous was liberated
from its sensual incarnation in the body through the agency of the
divine Nous, it soared aloft in unity with this consubstantial agent.
This unitary nature of the divine is the redemptive content of gnosis.

In the pattern common to the late Hellenistic gnosis, the visionary revelation of Poimandres includes an elaborate cosmogony, a
parallel anthropogony, and a concluding description of the final redemptive transcendence of the cosmos by the soul. The cosmogony,
reminiscent in places of the creation story in Genesis, opens with a
visionary and undifferentiated brilliance, identified by Poimandres as
the Intellect [*Nous*], the God, out of which devolved lower reality:

After a while, a fearful and terrifying darkness gradually appeared,
forcing its way down, rolling and twisting, so that I compared it with
a snake. Then the darkness was changed into a kind of moist Physis

[in Greek, nature], and fell into inextricable confusion, exuding
smoke as if from a fire, and emitting an indescribable voice as if in
lament.   *CH* I, 4

This devolved dark and moist nature is an image of the primal chaos
("inextricable confusion"). In a further differentiation of the pre-exist-
ent Light, the seer beholds "the Light, consisting of innumerable
forces which had now become a limitless cosmos" (*CH* I, 7), and
which Poimandres revealed was the "archetypal form, which exists
before the Limitless beginning" (*CH* I, 8).

When the masculine Logos or Son of God descends from the
Primal divine Light/Nous to have intercourse with the feminine earth/
watery substance below, the ordered world results. The Logos also
generates the Demiurge, who fashions the celestial system out of the
airy and fiery substance that had risen up from the lower nature. The
creatures of the earth, of the air, and of the sea emerged from the
animation of the spheres by the Demiurge and from their influence
upon the elements. In hermetic thought, the creatures who inhabit
this cosmic system were understood as components generated by this
system and consequently were totally dominated by its rule of
heimarmenē (*CH* I, 9).

The divine Light/Nous then created the Primal Anthropos, "a
being like himself." This Primal Anthropos, desiring to create (like
his brother the Demiurge), descended through the celestial realm. As
he descended, he acquired a share of the nature of each of the planetary spheres:

> When he entered the sphere of the demiurge where he was to re-
> ceive all authority, he observed the creative work of his brother,
> and the Administrators were pleased with him, and gave him a
> share of his own area.   *CH* I, 13

The characteristics of the planetary Administrators are detailed in a
later description of redemptive ascent, whereby the redeemed succes-
sively relinquish these planetary influences:

> And so man presses upward through the system of spheres. In the
> first sphere he leaves behind the ability to wax and wane; in the
> second the cunning of evil, from now on an ineffective trickery; in
> the third sphere, the deception of covetousness, which henceforth is
> ineffective; in the fourth, overbearing boastfulness, now a failure; in
> the fifth, frivolous audacity and rashness; in the sixth, evil desire for

wealth, henceforth inoperative; and in the seventh, the malicious lie. Then, stripped of all that lent the forces of the system of spheres their effect, man, who now possesses (only) his own strength, enters the Physis of the Ogdoas (Eighth), and sings hymns of praise to the Father together with the creatures (there). *CH* I, 25–26

This acquisition of planetary characteristics by descending through their spheres is an astrological principle that accounted for the influence of the planets over human existence. Hermeticism sought escape from the astrological claims of the planetary powers through practices that negated their influence.

In a second stage of fall, Anthropos broke through the celestial realm and thus "showed the beautiful form of God to the lower *Physis* [Nature]." They were united and the human condition was initiated:

> For this reason, man, unlike all other creatures on earth, is dual in nature: mortal in the body, but immortal through the real Anthropos. Though he is immortal and possesses authority over all things, he undergoes the fate of mortals in being subject to Destiny [*heimarmenē*]. *CH* I, 15

Fallen existence ruled by *heimarmenē* might be overcome through gnosis. In answer to the question "How shall I attain to Life?" Poimandres replies: "Let the Man who has Intellect [Nous] recognize himself." This same gnostic admonition to self-knowledge is expressed in another of the hermetic tractates in the alchemical image of the great crater or basin of Nous, sent by God, together with a messenger who proclaimed to all who would hear:

> baptize yourself in this crater, if you are able, believing that you shall ascend to the One who sent down the crater. *CH* IV, 4[29]

In one of the great texts in the history of religions, the thirteenth tractate of the *Corpus Hermeticum,* an attempt is made to describe the nature of this ascendant rebirth by forming "mental images no longer in the shape of three-dimensional corporeality" (*CH* XIII, 13).[30]

Gnostic and hermetic thought generally offered hope to those who experienced this world as oppressive in terms of the very assumptions of that world. Far from a nihilistic view of human existence, as it is usually characterized,[31] gnostic thought expressed a bold challenge to a view of human existence mastered by the material world and its universal claim of fate—a challenge that anticipated the Renaissance humanistic ideal of mastery over the world through knowledge of its universal natural laws. The hermetic texts greatly influenced Italian Renaissance thought with their translation into Latin by Marsilio Ficino in 1463.[32]

The Patriarchal Challenge

The third-century Christian Father Hippolytus wrote of the Eleusinian Mysteries that

> in the course of the night, the hierophant at Eleusis in the midst of a brilliant fire celebrating the Great and Unspoken Mysteries, cries and shouts aloud saying, "Holy Brimo has borne a sacred child Brimos," that is, the mighty gave birth to the mighty ones.
>
> *Haer.* V, 3[33]

Although Hippolytus was surely mistaken in his historical understanding of what had occurred during the Eleusinian initiation,[34] the meaning of his report from late antiquity is clear. From the discourse of the Mysteries, constellated around the feminine principle, emerged the divine son, who came in his maturity to rule over a new understanding of existence from his otherworldly throne beyond the cosmos as the supreme, spiritual Father of Light.

The discursive strategy of late Hellenistic gnosis represented a complete revaluing and reversal of the assumptions of Hellenistic religion. As the feminine principle of nature was mythologized, first as the traditional and beneficent Earth Mother of piety, and then as the transformative but capricious Tyche/Fortuna and her counterparts among the Mystery deities, and finally as the oppressive/chaotic rule of *heimarmenē,* masculine patterns of transcendence emerged in response and thus in challenge to her progressively perceived negative rule.

Notes

1. Robert Haardt, *Gnosis, Character and Testimony,* trans. J. F. Hendry (Leiden: E. J. Brill, 1971), pp. 167–176.

2. Franz Cumont, *Astrology and Religion Among the Greeks and Romans*, trans. J.B. Baker (New York: Dover, 1960), pp. 40–41, 97.

3. J. L. E. Dreyer, *A History of Astronomy from Thales to Kepler* (New York: Dover, 1953), pp. 203–204.

4. David Ulansey associates Hipparchus's discovery with the origins of Mithraism in the first century B.C.E. See *Mithras and Perseus: Mithraic Astronomy and the Anatolian Perseus-Cult,* Doctoral Dissertation, Princeton University, 1984, pp. 219–230.

5. Robert Pierce Casey, (trans.), *The Excerpta ex Theodoto of Clement of Alexandria* (London: Christophers, 1934).

6. See, for example, the opening lines of *The Gospel of Thomas* (*NHC* II, 2) and *The Book of Thomas* (*NHC* II, 7).

7. Kurt Rudolf, *Gnosis: The Nature and History of Gnosticism,* 2nd ed., trans. Robert McL. Wilson (San Francisco: Harper & Row, 1983), pp. 210, 293.

8. Rudolf, pp. 207, 291.

9. Rudolf, pp. 54–55.

10. Jonathan Z. Smith, *Map is Not Territory: Studies in the History of Religion* (Leiden: E. J. Brill, 1978), p. *x*.

11. Rudolf, pp. 9–30.

12. Rudolf, pp. 34–52.

13. A number of these texts have been identified as belonging to such a "Sethian" text group, including:

> *The Apocryphon of John,* the importance to Gnostic circles of which is indicated by the discovery of three separate copies at Nag Hammadi: *NHC* II, 1; III, 1; and IV, 1, in addition to a previously discovered version in the Berlin Codex 2 (see Rudolf, p. 28) and parallels in Irenaeus, *Haer.* I, 29.
>
> *Hypostasis of the Archons: NHC* II, 4
> *Gospel of the Egyptians: NHC* III, 2; IV, 2
> *Apocalypse of Adam: NHC* V, 5
> *Three Steles of Seth: NHC* VII, 5
> *Zostrianos: NHC* VIII, 1
> *Melchizedek: NHC* IX, 1
> *Thought of Norea: NHC* IX, 2
> *Marsanes: NHC* X, 1
> *Allogenes: NHC* XI, 3
> *Trimorphic Protennoia: NHC* XIII, 1

14. For a discussion of the problems concerning the existence of a Sethian Gnosticism, see Hans-Martin Schenke, "Das sethianische System nach Nag-Hammadi-Handschriften," in P. Nagel (ed.), *Studia Coptica* (Berlin: Akademie, 1974), pp. 165–173; and Bentley Layton (ed.), *The Rediscovery of Gnosticism,* vol. 2: *Sethian Gnosticism* (Leiden: E. J. Brill, 1981), especially Frederik Wisse, "Stalking Those Elusive Sethians," pp. 563–576;

Hans-Martin Schenke, "The Phenomenon and Significance of Gnostic Sethianism," pp. 588–616; and Discussions 3 and 5, pp. 578–587, 662–670.

15. Birger A. Pearson, "Seth in Gnostic Literature," in Layton, vol. II, pp. 472–514: 489.

16. "Discussion," in Layton, vol. II, p. 561; see also A. F. J. Klijn, *Seth in Jewish, Christian and Gnostic Literature* (Leiden: E. J. Brill, 1977).

17. Rudolf, p. 322; Gilles Quispel, "Valentinian Gnosis and the *Apocryphon of John*," in Layton, vol. 1, pp. 118–132. The texts from the Nag Hammadi discovery, which are grouped with the Valentinian tradition include the following:

The Gospel of Truth: NHC I, 3
The Treatise on Resurrection: NHC I, 4
Tripartite Tractate: NHC I, 5
The Gospel of Philip: NHC II, 3
A Valentinian Exposition: NHC XI, 2

18. Rudolf, p. 325.

19. Alexander Roberts and James Donaldson (eds. and trans.), *The Ante-Nicene Fathers* (orig. pub. 1885), (Grand Rapids, Mich.: Eerdmans, 1980–1985), vol. I.

20. Gilles Quispel, "Gnosis and Time," in Joseph Campbell (ed.), *Man and Time: Papers from the Eranos Yearbooks,* vol. 3, trans. Ralph Manheim and R. F. C. Hull (New York: Pantheon Books, 1957), pp. 38–84.

21. Rudolf, pp. 211–212, 270–272; Elaine Pagels, *The Gnostic Gospels* (New York: Random House, 1979).

22. Rudolf, p. 336.

23. Rudolf, p. 218.

24. Ron Cameron and Arthur J. Dewey (eds. and trans.), *The Cologne Mani Codex: "Concerning the Origin of His Body* " (Missoula, Mont.: Scholars Press, 1979), parts I–III. Parts IV–V, ed. by A. Henrichs and L. Koenen in *Zeitschrift für Papyrologie und Epigraphik* 32 (1978), pp. 87–199; English trans. R. Cameron and A. J. Dewey, forthcoming. See also A. Henrichs, "Literary Criticism of the Cologne Mani Codex," and L. Koenen, "From Baptism to the Gnosis of Manichaeism," in Layton, vol. II, pp. 724–733, 734–756.

25. Hans Jonas, *The Gnostic Religion,* 2nd ed. (Boston: Beacon Press, 1963), pp. 206–209; Rudolf, pp. 329–332.

26. Rudolf, pp. 374–376.

27. The following summary follows Jonas, pp. 209–236, and Rudolf, pp. 336–339.

28. Trans. in Haardt, pp. 333–334.

29. Trans. in Robert M. Grant, (ed.), *Gnosticism* (New York: Harper, 1961), pp. 220–223.

30. Trans. in Grant, pp. 226–233.

31. Jonas, "Epilogue: Gnosticism, Nihilism and Existentialism," pp. 320–340.

32. Francis A. Yates, *Giordano Bruno and the Hermetic Tradition* (New York: Random House, 1969), and Antonio G. Bianco, "Hermetism: A Bibliographical Approach", *Aufstieg und Niedergang der Römischen Welt* II, 17. 4 (Berlin and New York: Walter de Gruyter, 1984), pp. 2240–2281.

33. Trans. in George E. Mylonas, *Eleusis and the Eleusinian Mysteries* (Princeton, N.J.: Princeton University Press, 1961), p. 306.

34. Mylonas, pp. 306–310.

Selected Bibliography

Texts

R. Cameron and A. J. Dewey (eds. and trans.), *The Cologne Mani Codex: "Concerning the Origin of His Body"* (Missoula, Mont.: Scholars Press, 1979).

Robert M. Grant (ed.), *Gnosticism.* (New York: Harper, 1961).

Robert Haardt, *Gnosis: Character and Testimony,* trans. J. F. Hendry (Leiden: E. J. Brill, 1971.)

A. D. Nock and A.-J. Festugière (eds. and French trans.), *Corpus Hermeticum* (Paris: Société d'Edition "Les Belles Lettres," 1954–1960.)

James M. Robinson (ed.), *The Nag Hammadi Library* (San Francisco: Harper & Row, 1977).

Walter Scott, *Hermetica* (London: Dawsons, 1968), is the only complete English translation of the *Corpus Hermeticum,* based unfortunately on an unreliable text.

Studies

Ugo Bianchi (ed.), *The Origins of Gnosticism,* Colloquium of Messina, April 13–18, 1966 (Leiden: E. J. Brill, 1967).

F. C. Burkitt, *The Religion of the Manichees* (Cambridge: Cambridge University Press, 1925).

John Dart, *The Laughing Savior* (San Francisco: Harper & Row, 1976).

R. M. Grant, *Gnosticism and Early Christianity,* 2nd ed. (New York: A. R. Mowbray, 1966).

Henry A. Green, *The Economic and Social Origins of Gnosticism* (Atlanta, Ga.: Scholars Press, 1985).

Charles W.. Hedrick and Robert Hodgson, Jr. (eds.), *Nag Hammadi, Gnosticism, and Early Christianity* (Peabody, Mass.: Hendrickson, 1986).

Hans Jonas, *The Gnostic Religion,* 2nd ed. (Boston: Beacon Press, 1963), is the classic study in English.

Bentley Latyon (ed.), *"The Rediscovery of Gnosticism, Proceedings of the International Conference on Gnosticism at Yale,* New Haven, Connecticut, March 28–31, 1978, 2 vols. (Leiden: E. J. Brill, 1980–1981).

Elaine Pagels, *The Gnostic Gospels* (New York: Random House, 1979).

Kurt Rudolph, *Gnosis: The Nature and History of Gnosticism,* trans. and ed. Robert McL. Wilson (San Francisco: Harper & Row, 1983), is an excellent, up-to-date survey.

David M. Scholer, *Nag Hammadi Bibliography: 1948–1969* (Leiden: E. J. Brill, 1971), up-dated annually in *Novum Testamentum.*

Geo Widengren, *Mani and Manichaeism,* Eng. trans. (New York: Holt, Rinehart, 1965).

Robert Mcl. Wilson, *The Gnostic Problem* (London: A. R. Mowbray, 1958).

Conclusion:
Hellenistic Religion
as System

Questions of coherence may well be asked of the profuse religious data from the Hellenistic period. For example, was the worship of Demeter in Eleusis the same as or similar to that in Corinth or Syracuse? Why is Isis identified with Demeter in Apuleius's *The Golden Ass* but presented as antithetic to Atargatis, with whom she is elsewhere identified in Hellenistic sources? What was the relation of the universalized cult of Isis to her native worship in Egypt?[1] What accounts for the seemingly fortuitous and bizarre identification of such differing deities as Yahweh and Dionysus? Was there any coherent tradition of Dionysus or of Orpheus? And what of those religious formations documented from the Hellenistic period but not discussed in this book—for example, the piety accorded the emperors[2] or the Mysteries of the Cabiri at Samothrace?[3] What of the notion of demonic beings, which one interpreter considers so useful "that it is . . . impossible to imagine the description of [Greek] popular beliefs . . . without it?"[4] Or the crucial contributions of the Middle Platonists?[5] Or of apocalyptic Judaism, which many scholars consider "the Mother of all Christian theology."[6]

Rather than attempting a survey of all relevant data, this book has attempted to suggest something of the complexity of religious data in the Hellenistic period by introducing a rather traditional catalogue of religious formations that occurred during this age. In addition, it has attempted to describe a Hellenistic world in which certain principles operated to organize available religious conventions, and to introduce that world through some of its major religious formations.

The Hellenistic world was a world in transformation, a transformation characterized primarily by the general acceptance of a magnified spatial distribution by the end of the fourth-century B.C.E. The Ptolemaic cosmological revolution established a universal, hierarchically differentiated architecture of the cosmos in place of traditional, regionally centered topographies of the world. Coincident with this cosmological revolution, the conquests of Alexander successfully internationalized these geographies, challenging thereby the traditional social conventions of political identity with cosmopolitan aspirations. These wider distributions in the physical and political conditions of existence signaled also an enlargement of mind with increased possibilities for inspiration and discernment, but also for sophistry, folly and extravagance.

The effects of Hellenistic cosmological universalism, political internationalism, and widened cultural and intellectual possibilities together raised new questions of individual existence. The ethical concerns of Hellenistic philosophy, exemplified in literature by the labyrinthian wanderings of Apuleius's Lucius, replaced the classical cosmological and metaphysical certainties of Plato and Aristotle concerning the order of things. These Hellenistic transformations all generated the question reportedly asked of Jesus by an anonymous Everyman: "What must I do?" (Mark 10:17).

Hellenistic religions belonged to their world, and like that world were in transformation: from piety to mystery to gnosis. Local practices were adapted but not eclipsed by later religious formations, and formerly alien practices were enfolded into Hellenistic cosmopolitanism. The Mysteries, for example, practiced divination to establish the presence of the wayward goddess, and gnosis not only incorporated magical formulae but refined the gnosis of mystery teaching for its esoteric thought. Late antiquity witnessed the simultaneity of all three of these discursive strategies of existence even within a single text, as illustrated by the hermetic tractates.

The simultaneity of these diverse discursive and cultic practices has been termed syncretism. Despite the fact that it vividly describes a Hellenistic religion in transformation, however, the notion of syncretism does not suffice as an explanation of the transformations themselves.[7] The Hellenistic borrowings of religious strategies, one from another, and their influences upon one another, were not arbitrary responses to a situation of cultural interaction, which itself requires explanation beyond military conquest and cultural imposition.

The final book of Apuleius's *The Golden Ass* offers what is generally considered to be the classic example of Hellenistic religious syncretism, and the self-description of the goddess Isis in this book has been identified as "the syncretistic formula of union": "manifested alone and under one form of all gods and goddesses . . . my name, my divinity is adored throughout all the world, in divers manners, in variable customs, and by many names" (*Met.* XI, 5).[8] However, the identification of various deities in Book XI, 5 of Apuleius's novel, and in the Hellenistic world generally, is better understood as a sympathetic collage of normally discrete goddesses[9] who represent good fortune in the face of ill. Plutarch's understanding of syncretism as a coherent system of relationships defined by resemblance and organized by the play of sympathy and antipathy better explains the religious situation of the Hellenistic world than does the political sense of syncretism.

Hellenistic thought was characterized by its proclivity to systemize, a trait inherited from the classical Greeks. Already, Homer and Hesiod had organized a bewildering array of deities into a comparatively coherent system.[10] This Greek genius for compilation and systemization is exemplified in Hellenistic culture by the astronomical syllabus of Ptolemy, the oneiromantic taxonomy of Artemidorus, the alchemical reflections of Zosimos, the literary compendia of magicians, Christians, Jews, Orphics, and Gnostics, and the competing religious propaganda of the various mystery traditions. From this perspective too, the rich data of Hellenistic religious formations are comprehensible, not as the arbitrary product of a capricious syncretism but as the product of a coherent world system.

A coherent world order was articulated by both Greek philosophical and religious thought through a grammar of fate, the cosmological or natural and universal structure of an order of things constructed upon a system of oppositions between antipathetic determinism and sympathetic possibility. Already by the end of the nineteenth century, in which a Hellenistic age was first defined, it had been proposed that the gnostic teachings of late antiquity were directed against a deterministic rule of fate, that is, the uncontested sovereignty of astrological *heimarmenē*.[11] But concern with the rule of fate in the Hellenistic world was not limited to the anticosmic protest of late antiquity, nor was the notion of fate limited to the view of an oppressive *heimarmenē*. The Hellenistic structure of fate itself was in transformation along with the transitory world it articulated.

The Hellenistic notion of fate developed from the classical Greek assumption of a natural or cosmic order of things, expressed by *moira*. [12] This classical order of things was reconceived in the Hellenistic age in accordance with the new structures of Ptolemaic cosmology. Expressing the Hellenistic concern with ethics, fate was bifurcated, according to her ambiguous or assured character, into sub- and superlunar realms of activity. The ordered and ordering *Agathē Tychē* of the apparently stable heavens finally became perceived as the deterministic *heirmarmenē* of late antiquity. [13] These transformations and revaluations in the grammar of fate provided the systemic basis for the religions of the Hellenistic world and for the coherent structure underlying and shaping their sociohistorical expression (see Figure 3).

Several strategies of existence were employed in relation to the sovereignty of fate during the Hellenistic period. [14] An early and enduring response was the Hellenistic adaptation of traditional piety with its classical assumptions of a natural order of things and its repertoire of techniques for discerning that order. One technique, characteristic of some philosophical thought, was rational inquiry into the assumed natural order. This philosophical response is illustrated by Plutarch, who argued that what separates humans from lower forms of life is "Prometheus or, in other words, the power to think and reason" (*Peri Tychē* 3). For Plutarch and the philosophical position he represented, fate is a power that rules only animals and those who are unthinking. Mind and reason separate humans from the animals, according to Plutarch, and it is precisely this Promethean power to think and to reason that gives to humans their freedom from the rule of fate. [15]

More accessible to the populace was prognosis, or knowledge of the fated natural order, for which Stoicism offered a philosophical basis by advocating an existence in sympathetic harmony with the natural order (*heimarmenē*). As a universal or cosmological alternative, nowhere was prognosis more compelling to the Hellenistic imagination than as astrology. Ptolemy contrasted the unchangeability of the observable and regular motions of the superlunar celestial realm with the unpredictable, apparently chance, changes in the sublunar, terrestrial world. By contemplating the empirical order of celestial reality, he deemed it

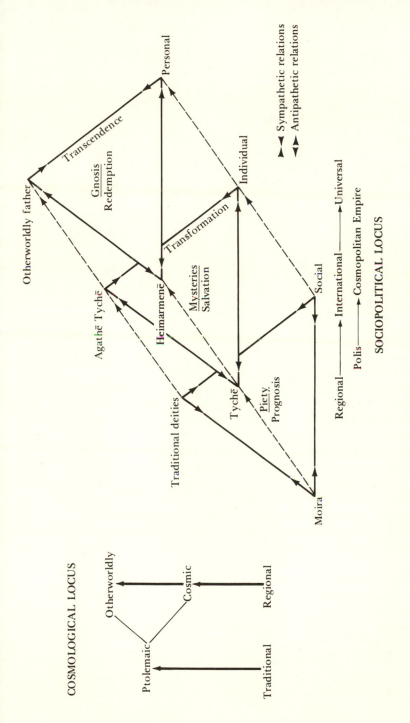

Figure 3. Hellenistic Religious System

COSMOLOGICAL LOCUS

Otherworldly

Cosmic

Regional

Ptolemaic

Traditional

SOCIOPOLITICAL LOCUS

Regional ——→ International ——→ Universal

Polis ——→ Cosmopolitan Empire

Personal

Otherworldly father

Transcendence

Gnosis
Redemption

Individual

Transformation

Agathē Tychē

Heimarmenē

Mysteries
Salvation

Social

Traditional deities

Tychē

Piety
Prognosis

Moira

Sympathetic relations
Antipathetic relations

possible to know the external effects of this cosmic order upon the seemingly fortuitous condition of human existence.

Divination thus shared with philosophy the assumption that there is order within the bounded cosmic order of things, and that this order is knowable, whether by the exercise of reason or through the practice of divinatory technique. Knowledge of this order established at-homeness in the Hellenistic expanse of sociopolitical possibilities, an order mythologically presided over by the traditional deities.

A second response to the rule of fate is exemplified by the Hellenistic Mysteries, in which an alienation of cosmic proportions replaced the local uncertainties previously addressed by pietistic practice. Pindar already hinted at this transition from piety to mystery practice when he prayed:

> Daughter of Zeus the Deliverer! thou saving goddess Fortune [*soteira Tychē*]! I pray thee. . . . But never yet hath any man on earth found a sure token sent from heaven to tell him how he shall fare in the future, but warnings of events to come are wrapped in gloom.   *Ol.* 12, 1–9

Thus Pindar suggests what Apuleius later made clear, that in the cosmopolitan world, divination does not satisfy.

Whereas philosophy and prognosis assumed a discernable natural order, the Mysteries assumed a terrestrial deficiency of order into which the cult deity revealed her celestial providence through soteriological initiation. Hellenistic mystery discourse assumed the ethical differentiation between *Tychē,* a personification of the Ptolemaic view of deficiency in the terrestrial or sublunar realm, and *Agathē Tychē,* the personification of the celestial or superlunar order of things. Fate was not simply the personification of a cosmic order of things; she had a negative side to be overcome in sympathetic relation with her positive nature, ritualized as a soteriological rebirth into the providential care of a sympathetic *Agathē Tychē.* It was only fate mythologized as the various savior goddesses, who was able to intercede on behalf of humans in the face of a capricious fate. With the Ptolemaic differentiation of the bounded cosmos and the consequent immigration of the traditional along with the newly naturalized deities to the celestial realm, access to a divinely sanctioned but now distant order was perceived as an even more fortuitous and individual affair.

The diverse responses that shared the characterization of "mystery" addressed the broadest spectrum of Hellenistic social situations. As there was in antiquity "no ideology other than what we call 'religion',"[16] mystery discourse established sociopolitical identity for the alienated individual, whether rural (Eleusinian) or urban (Isaic), male (Mithraic) or female (traditional Dionysian), ethnic (Jewish) or catholic (Christian), ecstatic (Dionysian) or bureaucratic (Mithraic), or exclusive (Jewish, Christian) or nonexclusive in some combination or juxtaposition.

The strategies of philosophy, prognosis, and providence all shared an essentially positive view of the world and sought to secure an at-homeness within its cosmic boundaries. In the face of an experienced deficiency in human existence, an order was assumed to exist within the bounded cosmos which by one practice or another was available to human knowing.

By late antiquity, the centrifugal force of Hellenistic expansion extended the locus of deficiency to the outer bounds of the cosmos itself. The necessary conclusion to this cosmic revaluation was that the totality of the finite cosmos, together with its predominately feminine attributes, was considered to be deficient. The gnostic and hermetic traditions mythologically expressed their view of a defective, feminine cosmos by the cosmogonic fall of Sophia, and their anticosmism as the resulting rule of *heimarmenē*.

In the face of late antique anticosmism, a masculine otherworldly alternative to fate emerged. Rejection of this-worldly existence in favor of a vertical relation to otherworldly and redemptive origins radically reconceived the distribution of order wholly in terms of the Ptolemaic hierarchical architecture of existence. As opposed to the mystery reintegration of the individual into some sort of ideal spiritual society, gnosis was a completely inner or personal strategy of existence, rejecting even individual bodily requirements. In the myth of revelatory ascent, the masculine redeemers of Mithraism, Christianity, and gnostic myth charted a "Way" through the celestial spheres of this-worldly determininsm for the faithful to follow in their own transcendence of *heimarmenē* and final reunion with the otherworldly Father Deity.

A masculine principle of order had been posited as early as the fabled heroic tradition of classical Greece. But Greek society was characterized by a strong matriarchal dominance that simultaneously encouraged and frustrated this heroic ideal.[17] Even in the patriarchal superstructure of Olympus, the goddesses were more intimately involved in the lives of men than were the gods.

Similarly, the patriarchal challenge of the late Hellenistic era was only partially successful. The Pauline redeemer Christ became subordinated in Christian theology to the synoptic Gospels' portrayal of

Christ as savior; and by the second century, Christianity had assumed many of the forms and practices of the mystery cults. This established, orthodox Christianity successfully conquered Mithraism, even constructing churches on the ruins of desecrated Mithraic sanctuaries, and effectively repressed Christian Gnosticism as heresy.

It was not until the Renaissance rediscovery of the classical world, mediated by Hellenistic culture, that the patriarchal challenge so forcefully mounted by Paul and the gnostic traditions was fully realized. The most explicit paradigm for the success of this challenge was the Protestant Reformation, which was grounded in Pauline theology and which finally expunged Christianity of its central feminine symbolism: its spiritual reorientation toward a transcendent godhead replaced the sacramental immanence mediated by the Mother Church; the centrality of the pulpit with its intellectual icon of book and word replaced the sacrificial altar, the center of the Catholic transformatory cult; and Mariology was renounced altogether.

It is not accidental that the Protestant Reformation and the Copernican revolution were contemporary transformations in the structure of the European world. For parallel to the final success of the patriarchal movement with its patterns of transcendence, the Copernican system described a boundless universe of infinite space, in which the inhabited earth itself is removed from the cosmic center. No longer was it possible to maintain an Augustinian separation between the transcendent City of God and the terrestrial City of Man. Rather, a quest for paradise throughout the possibilities of geographical expanse, both ancient and new, replaced the image of mystical ascent to an otherworldly locus.[18] In many ways, Alexander's cosmopolitan vision survives as the paradigm for the Renaissance and modern world as much as the inauguration of a Hellenistic age.

Notes

1. See the questions of interpretation raised by Jonathan Z. Smith, "Native Cults in the Hellenistic Period," *History of Religions* 11, 2 (1971), pp. 236–249.

2. See S. R. F. Price, *Rituals and Power: The Roman Imperial Cult in Asia Minor* (Cambridge: Cambridge University Press, 1984).

3. See C. Kerényi, "The Mysteries of the Kabeiroi," in Joseph Campbell (ed.), *The Mysteries: Papers from the Eranos Yearbooks,* vol. 2, trans. Ralph Manheim and R. F. C. Hull (New York: Pantheon, 1955), pp. 32–63.

4. Walter Burkert, *Greek Religion,* trans. John Raffan (Cambridge,

Mass.: Harvard University Press, 1985), p. 179, also pp. 179–181, 331–332; Jonathan Z. Smith, "Towards Interpreting Demonic Powers in Hellenistic and Roman Antiquity," *Aufstieg und Niedergang der Römischen Welt* II, 16. 1 (Berlin and New York: Walter de Gruyter, 1978), pp. 425–439.

    5. John Dillon, *The Middle Platonists, 80 B.C. to A.D. 220* (Ithaca, N.Y.: Cornell University Press, 1977).

    6. James H. Charlesworth (ed.), *The Old Testament Pseudepigrapha,* vol. 1: *Apocalyptic Literature and Testaments* (Garden City, N.Y.: Doubleday, 1983), p. 3.

    7. Jonathan Z. Smith, "Wisdom and Apocalyptic," in *Map is Not Territory: Studies in the History of Religions* (Leiden: E. J. Brill, 1978), pp. 67–87: 67.

    8. J. Gwyn Griffiths, *Apuleius of Madauros: The Isis-Book* (*Metamorphoses Book XI*) (Leiden: E. J. Brill, 1975), p. 144.

    9. A. D. Nock has argued that the Hellenistic age is marked by the distinctiveness of its religions, by individual deities, and individual initiation. "Ruler-Worship and Syncretism," in Zeph Stewart (ed.), *Essays on Religion and the Ancient World,* vol. II (Cambridge, Mass.: Harvard University Press, 1972), pp. 557–558.

    10. H. Idris Bell, *Cults and Creeds in Graeco-Roman Egypt* (Chicago: Ares, 1975), p. 9.

    11. Wilhelm Anz, *Zur Frage nach dem Ursprung des Gnostizismus* (Leipzig: J. C. Hinrich, 1897), pp. 13, 56–57.

    12. See William Chase Greene, *Moira: Fate, Good, and Evil in Greek Thought* (Gloucester, Mass.: Peter Smith, 1968).

    13. Erich Neumann has described in terms of Jungian psychology similar stages in the transformation of the archetypal feminine: from elemental to transformative to oppressive. See *The Great Mother: An Analysis of the Archetype,* trans. Ralph Manheim, 2nd ed. (Princeton, N.J.: Princeton University Press, 1963).

    14. A.-J. Festugière suggests that one's principle of organization in examining so vast a topic ought not to begin with the peculiarities of the contents but with genetic conditions. See "Cadre de la mystique hellénistique," in *Aux sources de la tradition chretiénne: Mélanges offerts à Maurice Goguel* (Neuchatel and Paris: Delachaux and Niestlé, 1950), pp. 74–85.

    15. H. R. Patch, "The Tradition of the Goddess Fortuna in Roman Literature and in the Transitional Period," Smith College Studies in Modern Language, 3 (1922), p. 149.

    16. Christiano Grottanelli, "Archaic Forms of Rebellion and their Religious Background," in Bruce Lincoln (ed.), *Religion, Rebellion, Revolution* (New York: St. Martin's Press, 1985), pp. 15–45: 15.

    17. Philip E. Slater, *The Glory of Hera: Greek Mythology and the Greek Family* (Boston: Beacon Press, 1968).

    18. E. M. Butler, *The Myth of the Magus* (New York: Macmillan, 1948).

Index

DATE DUE